WITHDRAWN

THE JOHN DEWEY LECTURE

The John Dewey Lecture is delivered annually under the sponsorship of the John Dewey Society. The intention of the series is to provide a setting where able thinkers from various sectors of our intellectual life can direct their most searching thought to problems that involve the relation of education to culture. Arrangements for the presentation of the Lecture and its publication by Teachers College Press are under the direction of James M. Giarelli, Chairperson.

TITLES IN THE SERIES

Excellence in Public Discourse:
John Stuart Mill, John Dewey, and Social Intelligence
James Gouinlock

Building a Global Civic Culture:
Education for an Interdependent World
Elise Boulding

The Dialectic of Freedom
Maxine Greene

Educating for Intelligent Belief or Unbelief
Nel Noddings

Educating for
Intelligent Belief or Unbelief

NEL NODDINGS

TEACHERS
COLLEGE
PRESS

Teachers College, Columbia University
New York and London

19,95

Published by Teachers College Press, 1234 Amsterdam Avenue,
New York, NY 10027

Grateful acknowledgment is made to the following for permission to reprint the
material indicated:

"Dirge Without Music" by Edna St. Vincent Millay: From *Collected Poems*, Harp-
erCollins. Copyright © 1928, 1955 by Edna St. Vincent Millay and Norma Millay
Ellis. Reprinted by permission of Elizabeth Barnett, literary executor.

"The Impercipient" by Thomas Hardy: From *Collected Poems of Thomas Hardy*,
1925, Macmillan, New York.

Library of Congress Cataloging-in-Publication Data

Noddings, Nel.
    Educating for intelligent belief or unbelief / Nel Noddings.
       p.   cm.—(The John Dewey lecture)
    Includes bibliographical references and index.
    ISBN 0-8077-3272-9 (cloth : alk. paper).—ISBN 0-8077-3271-0
(paper : alk. paper)
    1. Religion in the public schools—United States. 2. Religion—
Study and teaching—United States. 3. Religious education—United
States. I. Title. II. Series.
LC405.N63 1993   93-19098
377'.1'0973—dc20

ISBN 0-8077-3272-9
ISBN 0-8077-3271-0 (pbk.)

Printed on acid-free paper
Manufactured in the United States of America
98 97 96 95 94 93   6 5 4 3 2 1

To Jane Wassam,
superb secretary and wise friend.

Contents

Foreword

In *Educating for Intelligent Belief or Unbelief*, an expanded version of her 1991 John Dewey Lecture, Nel Noddings probes the many ways in which children's questions about God and gods, existence, and the meaning of life can and should be integrated into life in classrooms and the real world of the public schools. As Robert Coles writes in the Spiritual Life of Children (1990),

> The child's "house has many mansions"—including a spiritual life that grows, changes, responds constantly to the other lives that, in their sum, make up the individual we call by a name and know by a story that is all his, all hers.

Like Dewey and Coles, Noddings displays the continuities between religious questions and experiences and those encountered in mathematics, science, literature, and social studies curricula. As Dewey argued over a lifetime of writing about education, experience is continuous—and a curriculum that aims at promoting more than technical facility at decoding symbols must be grounded in critical issues arising out of lived experiences. When Noddings writes that existential questions are the backbone of the curriculum and that critical thinking is not mere technique, but the outgrowth of engagement with such questions, she valorizes these same understandings.

Noddings makes no brief for religious belief or unbelief. Instead, her aim is to bring the domain of religious belief and unbelief into the light of day; to make questions of religious belief and unbelief a subject of inquiry, connected to the other qualities and moods of our experience that fund the changing and complicated stories of our humanness. When she writes of the particular affinities between questions of God, gods, and the ultimate and the work of mathematics and scientists, she reminds us of Dewey's view that "prayer is the 'seek and ye shall find,' the inquiry of science." When she writes of the relation between religion and the quest for community, a sense of belonging, Noddings reminds us of Dewey's view that democracy is the means by which "the encounter of God in man . . . becomes a living, present thing, having its ordinary and natural sense. This truth is brought down to life; its segregation removed; it is made a common truth enacted in all departments of action, not in one isolated sphere called religious."

While honoring this legacy, Noddings moves well beyond it through a careful and comprehensive analysis of the varieties of religious belief and unbelief, the miseducative qualities of fundamentalism in all its forms, and the problematic history of women and religious traditions. While always open to further inquiry and the spirit and substance of experimental teaching and self-directed learning, Noddings helps us frame a practical program of educating for intelligent belief and unbelief in contemporary schools.

Dewey once wrote that the educator is concerned with what does not exist. Whether we think of these matters in the vocabulary of the metaphysical, the supernatural, or as a nod to the pure contingency of lived experience, we ask only of our teachers and schools that they help us to connect our passions and problems to the words and images they present us as we try to compose a faithful accounting of the stories of our lives as they unfold along the way. Nel Noddings' *Educating for Intelligent Belief or Unbelief* is a worthy companion and valuable guide on this journey.

> *James M. Giarelli*
> *Chair, John Dewey Lecture Commission*

Acknowledgments

Besides recognizing a host of writers who have influenced me and whose works are cited in this book, I want to thank those who have made specific suggestions on the manuscript at various stages: Henry Alexander, René Arcilla, Byron Bland, Janet Chance, and Maxine Greene. I also thank the convenors and audiences of several invited lectures for their helpful feedback. Earlier versions of several chapters were presented as lectures: "Educating for Intelligent Belief or Unbelief" (Ch. 1), John Dewey Lecture at AERA; "The Nature of Gods" (Ch. 2), John Dewey Lecture at Teachers College, Columbia University; "Feminism and Religion" (Ch. 4), Nancy Rowell Jackman Distinguished Lecture, Mt. St. Vincent's College, Halifax, and the Leon and Thea Koerner Lecture, Simon Fraser University; "Talking to Students About Death, Immortality and Pessimism" (Ch. 5), Anna Funk Lockey Lecture, Millersville, PA; "Humanism and Unbelief" (Ch. 6), Butts Lecture, AESA.

Thanks also to family and friends for encouragement; to my former assistant, Nancy Baumann, for taking on more than her share of work so that I could finish this book; and to my present assistant, Elissa Hirsh, for entering final corrections, and to my secretary, Jane Wassam, for her usual competence and good humor.

Introduction

Intelligent believers and intelligent unbelievers are often closer in thought and spirit than intelligent and unintelligent believers. Michael Novak (1965) remarked on this odd affinity in his *Belief and Unbelief*. The theologian Hans Kung (1980), too, has commented:

> Yes to God? For many believers, this has not been obvious for a long time. No to God? Neither has this been obvious for a long time to unbelievers. (p. xxi)

Intelligent believers and unbelievers both suffer existential anxieties, harbor doubts, castigate religion for its role in social ills and oppression, and share ethical ideals. Through most of human history, questions about the existence and nature of gods, about the meaning of life, about the role of religion in societies, and about moral life with or without gods have been recognized as paramount in any examined life and, therefore, central to education. Even when the Enlightenment threatened to sweep gods away in a whirlwind of reason—even when Nietzsche credited human heroes with killing God—even in those heady days, recognized thinkers felt the need to say something of God or gods. Well into this century, the trend continued. John Dewey (1934), for example, rejected the theism of his earlier days but still felt the need to say something of God. He sought God in "the unity of all ideal ends arousing us to desire and action" (p. 42) and wrote, "It is this *active* relation between ideal and actual to which I would give the name 'God'" (p. 51). Even Bertrand Russell (1957) felt constrained to explain to the world why he was not a Christian.

It is only in the second half of this century that we find philosophers and educators ignoring religion entirely, and even now reasonable philosophers—such as Mary Midgley (1984)—warn that we cannot simply get rid of religion. While educational theorists have been ignoring religion as though the enlightenment project had succeeded, more and more people have actually returned to religion. One suspects that neither the new believers nor those who simply ignore religion are, for the most part, intelligent in their belief or unbelief.

What is meant by "intelligent" belief or unbelief? In using this term, I do not mean to suggest that belief or unbelief must be rational in the narrow sense. I am not referring to what might be called Rationality (capital R rationality)—a system of prescribed linear thinking or problem solving. Rationality in the broadest sense recognizes the longings of heart and soul and provides for them. An education for intelligent belief or unbelief puts great emphasis on self-knowledge, and that knowledge must come to grips with the emotional and spiritual as well as the intellectual and psychological. To believe without either the evidence required by scientists or the logic promoted by the scholastics is not irrational. But to believe without thinking through the questions that arise regularly in life—to merely accept or reject—is surely not intelligent. It is also unintelligent to ignore either the positive or negative side of religion. Education for intelligent belief or unbelief is as much education of the heart as it is education of the mind.

There is another reason to question my emphasis on belief. Christianity, it is said, focuses on belief more than most other religions do. Judaism, for example, places more importance on ritual and practice. Indeed, some people today ignore the religious nature of Judaism entirely. In a letter to the *Village Voice*, Nat Hentoff declared himself a "Jewish atheist." Responding to the June 9 (1992) issue, Warren Allen Smith of the Secular Humanist Society says that Hentoff cannot be a Jewish atheist any more than one could be a "black white." If he has given up religion, Smith writes, Hentoff should call himself a secular humanist. Hentoff's (1992) reply:

> I have now come full circle. Several rabbis once "excommunicated" me because I am for an independent Palestinian state. Now the secular humanists would censure me for calling myself Jewish. As I told the rabbis, I define myself, and it ain't nobody's business but my own. (Letters)

Perhaps Hentoff should settle for the label "existentialist." In any case, the Hentoff–Smith exchange illustrates the fascinating mixture of belief, culture, politics, logic, and passion that is conjured up by the word *religion*. Even though few religions besides Christianity use belief as a basic test, belief is clearly involved in all religions. People do not engage in rituals and practices without believing in something that gives these rituals and practices meaning. (At least, I am arguing here that such behavior would not be intelligent.)

There are also positive reasons for the emphasis on belief. Christianity is the name given to a set of religions that has had, and continues to have, the greatest influence on American culture, and American schoolchildren should be encouraged to examine this set of religions critically. Further, questions about belief are fundamental to education itself: What should I believe? On what grounds? To what ends? What obligations do I incur when I affirm certain beliefs? To whom do I tie myself? Finally, a focus on belief serves to delimit the discussion. My purpose is not to lay out a curriculum of comparative religion, and so I do not discuss religious art, music, architecture, or prayer. Neither do I discuss the number of believers in various religions or their geographic distribution. My purpose is to help parents and teachers think about appropriate responses to the kinds of questions all teenagers ask—explicitly or implicitly—and to think, further, about the questions all of us *should* ask if we want to be more whole individually and more tolerant and appreciative interpersonally.

I will argue that schools—public schools—should play a major role in educating for intelligent belief or unbelief. There is nothing in the establishment clause of the first amendment that prevents classroom instruction *about* religion (Levy, 1986). Further, so long as our presentations are balanced, I see no legal reason why various religious claims and critiques cannot be discussed in all their richness. This is not to say that everyone will agree that we should do this or that no vociferous voices will be raised in protest. The trend toward bland and boring curriculum has been aggravated by just such protests. To reverse the trend will require courage, sensitivity, and balance. In what follows, I hope to illustrate some of the possibilities.

Throughout the text, I have tried to demonstrate an approach that I believe to be legally, ethically, and pedagogically responsible. I rarely say, "I believe . . . " in connection with any statement on religion. Rather I say, "So-and-so has said," or "Many Christians believe . . . " (and then I quote particular writers). In most cases, highly controversial or passionate statements are followed by contrary opinions or reflective revisions. As I argue later in the book, teachers must try, for the sake of their students, to maintain pedagogical neutrality (Vandenberg, 1983). Such neutrality is not the same as moral neutrality. Even if I believe some attitude or practice is morally right and insist that students behave in accordance with my belief (on, say, racist language), I still have an obligation as a teacher to give reasons for my belief and to present cogent arguments—where they exist—against my own position.

With even the most meticulous pedagogical neutrality, the teacher will come through as a person. That glance, that raising of a finger, as Martin Buber put it, each conveys something. It is especially important, therefore, that teachers engage in the sort of critical exploration I describe here. If the material itself never reaches high school students, the attitude, wonder, faith, skepticism, and intelligence of their teachers might very well lead them to inquire on their own.

Educating for
Intelligent Belief or Unbelief

CHAPTER 1

Existential and Metaphysical Questions in the Classroom

People of all kinds—of all times and places—have asked questions about gods, existence, and the meaning of life. Cowboys riding the range on starry nights, mothers watching over children, astronomers gazing through telescopes at the heavens, philosophers pondering why there is something rather than nothing—all of us ask: Is there a God? Where did life come from? What is the meaning of life? The questions take a variety of forms, but at bottom they are universal.

In this chapter, I will suggest a few ways we can treat these questions in regular high school classes. A main purpose will be to show how much can be accomplished along these lines in mathematics and science classes. Although a complete course in religious thought would be a welcome addition to the curriculum, such a course is not necessarily the best way to emphasize our concern. When students hear about religious and moral issues in all of their regular classes, they are more likely to be persuaded that we really do regard these matters as important. Further, I want to challenge the long-standing assumption that mathematics should be taught as a totally separate, isolated set of skills and concepts. If I can convince readers that we can educate for intelligent belief or unbelief in mathematics classes, they may be convinced that we can do it anywhere!

In subsequent chapters, I will discuss the nature of gods and the possibility of spiritual progress; the desire to belong and the positive and negative aspects of religious affiliation; feminism and religion as part of the politics of religion; immortality, salvation, and pessimism; humanism; religious and secular ethics; and, finally, whether the kind of program I suggest here is at all feasible. Throughout, my purpose is to show how the serious treatment of religious topics can contribute to intellectual, moral, and emotional as well as spiritual development.

DOES GOD EXIST? ARE THERE GODS?

These questions are central to intelligent belief or unbelief. The question is usually cast in the first form: Does God exist? Few people are bold enough to ask the second, although some committed theists recognize the logical possibility of multiple gods (Gardner, 1983), and—as we will see in a bit—mathematical theorizing might convince us that the idea of many gods is more rational than that of one God.[1]

Mathematics classes are perfect settings for the exploration of this fascinating existential question. When students are introduced to rectangular coordinates and graphing, they should also hear something about their inventor, Rene Descartes, and his attempt to prove that God exists. They should hear that Descartes led a colorful life, that he was a fashionable dresser and engaged in swashbuckling adventure. He was adept at swordplay and ready to draw his sword when rowdies insulted him or the lady he was escorting. Dressed like one of the three musketeers, Descartes cut quite a figure (Bell, 1965).

Telling stories is a valuable technique not only for introducing religious and existential questions but for all teaching. Unfortunately, mathematics teachers rarely use stories, and their training is deficient in using narrative techniques, but this deficiency can be removed.

Swashbuckler, soldier, mathematician, Descartes also tackled the question of God's existence by reviving and polishing St. Anselm's "ontological" proof. The basic idea of the ontological proof is that God is conceived as the perfect entity, and a perfect entity must exist—otherwise it would not be perfect! The idea of perfection, that is, carries with it, of necessity, the provision that whatever is perfect must exist. Can students find anything wrong with this proof?

There should be nothing in the least offensive to either believers or unbelievers in this discussion. A great believer, the philosopher

---

[1]A note on style: Throughout this book, I capitalize God in the singular and use lower case for the plural, gods. No religious or theoretical significance attaches to this choice.

Immanuel Kant, showed convincingly that the proof demonstrates only the existence of a *concept* of perfection—not a perfect *entity*. But the failure of rational proof does not destroy the possibility of God's existence. Further, there is the possibility that God is not perfect and that the ontological proof is, thus, irrelevant. The possibility of an imperfect God will be considered in Chapter 2.

When students study probability, they should hear about the life of Pascal and another approach to the question: Does God exist? Pascal's interest in games of chance usually fascinates students, but they rarely hear how Pascal responded to Descartes's attempt to prove that God exists. Pascal rejected all attempts to prove God's existence, finding them not only mistaken but useless in persuading ordinary people. In keeping with his interest in games of chance, Pascal proposed instead a wager—one designed to induce commitment. Suppose you bet that God exists and live your life accordingly. If he does exist, what do you stand to gain? If he does not, what have you lost?

Thoughtful teachers should find the discussion of Pascal a good occasion to mention that Jews, in agreement with Pascal, do not regard God as a hypothesis to be proved. In rabbinical thought, far more argumentation involves human behavior and what God wants us to do than God's nature and existence. More will be said on this in Chapter 2.

If great believers have steadfastly exposed the errors in logical attempts to prove God's existence, great unbelievers have sometimes been almost persuaded by these same proofs. Bertrand Russell admitted to such a close call in his university days. But, later, asked whether he was never afraid of God's judgment for denying him, Russell (1963) responded:

> Most certainly not. I also deny Zeus and Jupiter and Odin and Brahma, but this causes me no qualms. I observe that a very large portion of the human race does not believe in God and suffers no visible punishment in consequence. And if there were a God, I think it unlikely that he would have such an uneasy vanity as to be offended by those who doubt His existence. (p. 200)

Listening to this, students may realize that some intelligent unbelievers express greater respect for a God whose existence they doubt than many believers who confess far more frail a God.

There have been amusing as well as serious attempts to prove God's existence. Mathematics students today are usually introduced to the word *algorithm* in computer science. They should hear about a mathematician, Leonard Euler, who was an extraordinary algorist or deviser of algorithms. Euler's proofs of God include the nonsense proof with which he humiliated the great French philosopher Diderot. Before the gathered court of Catherine the Great in Russia, Euler declared to Diderot: "Sir, $\frac{a + b^n}{n}$ = x, hence God exists; reply!" (Bell, 1965, p. 147). Poor Diderot was entirely at a loss. He, like many of today's students, was cowed by the reputation and authority of a great mathematician.

The existence of God or gods can be discussed in all classes, but it is especially fascinating to consider its inclusion in mathematics classes because students so rarely encounter anything there beyond the manipulation of mathematical symbols. One possible response from students might be that "only the old guys thought about this stuff." But Martin Gardner, whose delightful puzzles many students know, published his *Whys of a Philosophical Scrivener* in 1983 and grappled seriously with questions about God. Rudy Rucker (1982), too, mentions God in his discussion of the infinite. Indeed he uses a powerful idea from set theory, the Reflection Principle, to show that the Absolute (or God) cannot be a unity characterized by some unique powerful property. "According to the Reflection Principle," writes Rucker, "once one has an infinite Absolute, one must also have many [other] conceivable infinites as well" (p. 51). "Rationally," declares the mathematician, "the universe is a Many, but mystically it is a One" (p. 191). What escapes rational proof again and again pops up continually in human feeling. As Pascal (1662/1966) said, "The heart has its reasons of which reason knows nothing; we know this in countless ways" (p. 154).

Even the science-fiction classic, *Flatland* (Abbott, 1884/1952), can be used to discuss the existence and abode of God or gods. This fascinating little book gives teachers an opportunity to criticize the misogyny of the nineteenth century, the snobberies of classism, and the difficulties in conveying unfamiliar experiences to those who have not had them. Some time ago, I recommended *Flatland* to some of our mathematics intern-teachers. They responded by saying that they felt uncomfortable using a book that so degrades women. But, I protested, that is one of the very best reasons to use it! If we want to improve our students' thinking, we have to confront them with lively and well-expressed works that take objectionable as well as admirable positions. How better to introduce the topic of sexism in a math class?

Flatland, written in the 1880s, is a mathematical fantasy. It is the story of human-like geometrical figures who populate a two-dimensional land. Flatland is a rigidly hierarchical society in which many-sided polygons occupy the highest positions. Workers and soldiers are mere triangles, and generally they cannot escape their lowly inherited positions. Once in a great while a perfect equilateral triangle fathers a square, and upward mobility begins. Women in this society are line segments, portrayed as dangerous, talkative, and totally devoid of any hope for improvement in their lot. Not even by happy chance can they move up in society as an equilateral triangle might.

Because they are line segments—like needles—women are extremely dangerous. The law decrees separate entrances for them and insists that they issue a continual "peace-cry" so that unsuspecting males will always be aware of their presence. Further,

> Any female, duly certified to be suffering from St. Vitus's Dance, fits, chronic cold accompanied by violent sneezing, or any disease necessitating involuntary motions, shall be instantly destroyed. (1884/1952, p. 13)

Students will certainly be shocked by the misogyny of *Flatland*. But the tale is theological as well as mathematical and political. What might it be like for a Flatlander (a dweller in two dimensions) to experience the third dimension? For the square to whom the godlike cube appears, it is a spiritual experience. What would it be like for us to experience (not just posit) a fourth dimension? A commentator speaks in the preface to those "Spacelanders of moderate and modest minds who—speaking of that which is of the highest importance, but lies beyond experience—decline to say on the one hand, 'This can never be,' and on the other hand, 'It must needs be precisely thus, and we know all about it'" (Preface).

At the end of *Flatland*, students learn still more about political and religious oppression. The unfortunate narrator, an upstanding square in his society, is in prison for persisting in his heretical claim to have seen a cube and a sphere. He knows that he has been visited by three-dimensional beings, but in his psychic suffering, his faith in the visitations wavers.

> It is part of the martyrdom which I endure for the cause of Truth that there are seasons of mental weakness, when Cubes and Spheres flit away into the background of scarce-possible existences; when the Land of Three Dimensions seems almost as visionary as the Land of One or None; nay, when even this hard wall [a line, of course] that bars me from my freedom, these very tablets on which I am writing, and all the

substantial realities of Flatland itself, appear no better than the offspring
of a diseased imagination, or the baseless fabric of a dream. (1884/1952,
p. 103)

None of what I have described so far is meant to suggest that
each topic must be treated with the rigor of college mathematics or
philosophy. The idea is to acknowledge students' longing for connection and meaning, to show the vitality of mathematical thinkers and
thinking, to break away from the humdrum of the traditional curriculum. Now comes the perennial classroom question: "Can we cover
all the expected mathematics and this material too?" One answer to
this is that we probably could because we and our students would be
awake, involved, active. But even if we could not, so what? How
does the factor theorem stack up against the possible existence of
God?

WHERE DID I COME FROM?
HOW DID THE UNIVERSE START?

These questions intrigue scientists and theologians, cowboys and
gentlewomen, adults and children, believers and unbelievers. Listen
to Huckleberry Finn:

It's lovely to live on a raft. We had the sky, up there, all speckled with
stars, and we used to lay on our backs and look up at them, and discuss
about whether they was made or only just happened—Jim he allowed
they was made, but I allowed they happened; I judged it would have
took too long to *make* so many. Jim said the moon could a *laid* them;
well, that looked kind of reasonable, so I didn't say nothing against it,
because I've seen a frog lay most as many, so of course it could be done.
We used to watch the stars that fell, too, and see them streak down. Jim
allowed they'd got spoiled and was hove out of the nest. (Twain, 1885/
1982, p. 742)

In schools where *Huckleberry Finn* still appears, students will read
this passage in English class. But it should also be discussed in science classes. Here we should remind ourselves to challenge the wisdom—or, better, stupidity—of eliminating books that contain sexism
or racism. Even if *Huckleberry Finn* were guilty of racism (and it can
be argued that its message is antiracist), it would still be unwise to
ban it. Just as *Flatland* gives us an opportunity to discuss Victorian

sexism, so Huck's adventures with Jim provide an opportunity to discuss slavery, friendship, and morality.

In science classes, as teachers and students speculate about the creation of the universe and the origin of life, forms of the cosmological argument for the existence of God may arise. If everything has a cause, must not the universe itself have a cause? Does it not make sense to call this first cause "God?" Students, thinking hard, may see one of the difficulties: What, then, caused God? Hot on the heels of that question comes another: If God caused himself (herself, itself), then why couldn't the universe cause itself? With Spinoza and Einstein, some students might begin to define God as the self-creating power of the universe itself. The mystery remains.

The cosmological proof too must of course be regarded as a failure. Yet as Kant (1781/1966), that remarkable disprover-believer, wrote:

> Unconditioned necessity, which we so indispensably require as the last bearer of all things, is for human reason the veritable abyss. Eternity itself, in all its terrible sublimity . . . is far from making the same overwhelming impression on the mind; for it only *measures* the duration of things; it does not *support* them. We cannot put aside, and yet also cannot endure, the thought that a being, which we represent to ourselves as supreme amongst all possible beings, should as it were, say to itself: "I am from eternity to eternity, and outside me there is nothing save what is through my will, *but whence then am I?*" All support here fails us. (p. 409)

"Whence then am I?" If we are left without an answer to the question God asks itself, we may still try to answer it for ourselves, for we are finite creatures. As educators we have allowed ourselves to become embroiled in perennial battles over the teaching of evolution and creation. My own response is to teach both and in just the same way I have suggested for previous topics. I would teach both in science classes and everywhere else the topic might naturally arise. We do not have to say: This explanation is science, and that one is religion. Nor do we have to say: Here is truth, and there is myth. We need only present each in as full a context as time and interest allow. I will return to this example in Chapter 8.

But are not some explanations more adequate than others? Of course. It is a vital task of education to help students gather evidence, assess arguments, discriminate among authorities, construct counterarguments, and challenge claims. Education should also promote a tolerance for unavoidable ambiguity and an appreciation for subtle differences. Some creationists, for example, are very close in their beliefs to theistic evolutionists. Others—strict creationists and a conservative branch of progressive creationism (Numbers, 1986)—insist on the special and specific creation of all species. Description of evolution and creation should not leave students with the wrong notion that there are exactly two mutually exclusive realms of belief. Exploring a controversy of this sort is one way of helping students to see that it is intellectually irresponsible to discard or discount a person's beliefs or arguments by mere labeling. In a recent issue of *The New York Review of Books*, Tatyana Tolstaya (1991) commented on Robert Conquest's *The Great Terror*. Tolstaya remarked that Russia has an almost unbroken record of terror in the form of intolerance for nonconformity and that an ever-popular pattern of oppression has been destruction by category: Label persons, associate them with an unacceptable view, and justify their elimination or derision. Students should be aware how universal this technique is, even if it does not always culminate in physical destruction and ultimate terror.

Existential questions should form the organizing backbone of the curriculum, and they should be appropriate everywhere. We rob study of its richness when we insist on rigid boundaries between subject matters, and the traditional disciplinary organization makes learning fragmentary and—I dare say—boring and unnecessarily separated from the central issues of life.

While the present stultifying organization remains in place, however, we have to stretch it as best we can. The evolution–creation debates provide interesting material for history, science, and literature courses, but in each class discussion should be pushed well beyond the conventional boundaries. Students should certainly learn about the Scopes trial (and the dazzling verbal pyrotechnics of Bryan and Darrow), but they should also learn that—despite the overwhelming acceptance of evolution by scientists—there has been a recent considerable increase in the number of people who espouse creationism (Numbers, 1986). They should hear, too, that, even among thinkers who accept the general teachings of evolution, there are those who insist that some human attributes—language, for example (Chomsky, 1972)—represent true "emergents"—attributes without continuous links to the nonhuman animal kingdom. This notion challenges the generality of evolution's continuity hypothesis. The attempt to confine all topics within their proper disciplines works against the kind of understanding human beings long for—understanding with meaning for their personal lives.

Sometimes students want to know why life forms or physical objects (stars, in Huck's case) exist in such number and variety. (Sometimes the issue arises in a negative context: Why are there so many different insects, plant classifications, stars, and other things to learn about?) Here is an opportunity to talk about the principle of plentitude espoused by many thinkers, among them Plotinus, Augustine, and the mathematician Leibniz. According to those who embrace this principle, existence is a fundamental good and, in the Christian interpretation, God-the-creator has chosen out of love to give existence to the greatest range of possible forms. This discussion could arise in a science class; it could arise in a math class when Leibniz is mentioned as an inventor of calculus; it could arise in the study of Voltaire's *Candide* (in which Dr. Pangloss is a spoof on Leibniz's reference to this as "the best of all possible worlds"); it could arise in a history class where students might ask why the germs, lice, or rats causing plagues exist; and, of course, it could arise in an art class where students might see depictions of creation. The cover of *God and Nature* (Lindberg & Numbers, 1986), for example, displays a rare painting of God creating the world out of nothing.

Looking at a picture of God creating the world out of nothing raises an interesting question about the theological doctrine of creation *ex nihilo*. Does one have to believe in such creation, or are there other theological possibilities? Some process theologians today posit a creative force in addition to a being, God, who shapes and orders the universe. From this perspective, God is the most powerful being, but God does not have all the power; that is, other products of creativity have power that is not derived from God's. Theoretically, this is an important position because it helps to explain why there is evil in a world shaped by an all-good God. Practically, it is important because students need to know that many thoughtful, faithful people challenge basic beliefs and bits of dogma.

When students are exposed to mythology in literature classes, another opportunity arises to shatter conventional boundaries and break down false dichotomies. Some students might, understandably, be offended by the inclusion of biblical accounts of creation in *mythology*. Their religious beliefs are, for them, not myths. Here is an opportunity to induce more intelligent belief by describing the meaning of "myth" more deeply and fully. Paul Ricoeur (1969), for example, tells us that the power of myths actually grows as they lose their false logos. As their original explanatory power fades away, their symbolic power may grow, enriching the metaphorical language and range of meanings for people holding a diversity of basic beliefs.

Thus myths should not be associated with untruth but, rather, with timeless concerns given new meanings in new eras.

Instead of sharply separating religion and mythology (thereby omitting biblical creation stories except from courses on the Bible as literature), teachers might better simply present great *stories*. Here are great universal questions, and here are some of the ways people have answered them. The two creation stories in Genesis should be studied not only as literature but as an exercise in logic: Can they be made compatible? In Genesis 1, we are told, "So God created man in his own image, in the image of God created he him; male and female created he them" (I:27). But in Genesis 2, we find the well-known story of Eve's creation from Adam's rib. This story, it should be noted, appears right after mention of the penalty for eating fruit from the tree of knowledge. Eve's creation comes immediately on the heels of a forewarning of doom. What political purposes might have been served by emphasizing the second creation story over the first? Here students should be introduced to some of the powerful feminist writing on the subject. Merlin Stone (1976) describes the first Genesis story as compatible with earlier stories in which both man and woman were created simultaneously by the Goddess. But the second story—so eagerly embraced by both Hebrew and Christian traditions—ensures the subservience of women by suggesting a monumental inversion. Woman is now born of man; the familiar biological story is inverted. Stone comments:

> The Divine Ancestress was written out of reality. We are then informed that the woman so made . . . was presented as a gift to man, declaring and assuring her status—among those who accepted the myth—as the property of the male. (p. 220)

Nowhere in this discussion need teachers say, "Here's how it is" or "This is what intelligent people believe." All teachers should do is to provide access to the rich and numerous contemporary discussions of the creation myths. Every year in my course on Women and Moral Theory, I encounter highly intelligent graduate students (some in their forties!) who have never been exposed to these critiques. Their reaction is almost always anger—anger not only at traditional religion but even more at the faulty education that passed them clear through to graduate school in deplorable ignorance.

It is essential that such stories and their criticisms be taught. We talk perennially about teaching critical thinking but, too often, we settle for critical thinking as a bland (if powerful) set of techniques.

We forget that critical thinking is induced by tackling critical issues—issues that matter deeply to us. If we were serious about teaching critical thinking, we would use our own powers at it to find ways to do it despite the ravings of ideologues.

Students need to know that there are political and social, as well as religious and scientific, interests embedded in the questions: Where did I come from? How did the universe start? Recognizing this fact, feeling the stab of pain that every woman feels when she hears how her religious heritage has systematically abused her, one is still left with the question asked at the edge of the abyss: Whence then *am* I?

WHAT IS THE MEANING OF LIFE?

Perhaps no other existential question is more important to most people. Some never get to explore it in depth. Children in the Catholic faith learn that the purpose of life is "to know and love God . . . ," but since they rarely hear the notion discussed in "important" areas of schooling, they learn to compartmentalize their curiosity and, worse, their longings. Spiritual longing is semi-satisfied in ritual; existential longing is sacrificed to the pursuit of material goals. One starts with good grades, "solid" courses, the right schools, and proceeds to a good job. Inside, a small voice may continue to ask (in English, of course), Quo vadis? Quo vadis?

The meaning or purpose of life has to be sought in a context that recognizes death. Students should hear Edna St. Vincent Millay's (1928) "Dirge Without Music."

> I am not resigned to the shutting
>   away of loving hearts in the
>   hard ground.
> So it is, and so it will be, for so it has
>   been, time out of mind:
> Into the darkness they go, the wise and the
>   lovely. Crowned
> With lilies and with laurel they go;
>   but I am not resigned.
>
> Lovers and thinkers, into the earth with you.
> Be one with the dull, the indiscriminate dust.
> A fragment of what you felt, of what you knew,
> A formula, a phrase remains,—but the best is lost.

> The answers quick and keen, the honest look, the
>   laughter, the love,—
> They are gone. They are gone to feed the roses.
>   Elegant and curled
> Is the blossom. Fragrant is the blossom. I know.
>   But I do not approve.
> More precious was the light in your eyes than all
>   the roses in the world.
>
> Down, down, down into the darkness of the grave
> Gently they go, the beautiful, the tender, the kind;
> Quietly they go, the intelligent, the witty, the brave.
> I know. But I do not approve. And I am not resigned.

For some, such thinking leads to theism. Martin Gardner (1983) uses Millay's last verse to introduce a chapter entitled "Why I Am Not Resigned." Others are led to thoughts of an evil God, and students should hear about this possibility; still others to the conviction that the universe is meaningless—life itself absurd. The "Dirge" comes to us from the same poet who wrote, "Euclid alone has looked on beauty bare," so once again we have access to her thought in mathematics class—not only in literature class. Indeed the most dramatic effect might be obtained in mathematics class, because the poems would not be presented for formal analysis but for connection—to respond to a longing too often ignored. What did Euclid leave behind long after his body fed the roses? What did Millay leave behind? What will you leave behind?

Students should have opportunities to discuss death and its connection to the meaning of life. John Silber (1989), with whom I disagree on most things, says that education should expose them "to what is true, to a confrontation with what is real" (p. 5). He wants children to be acquainted with the reality principle—with the "ever-present possibility of death" (p. 8). Indeed, the recommendation to induce the awareness of death in children appears on the second page of his book. His descriptions and prescriptions illustrate—worse, endorse—dramatically much of what is wrong with traditional, patriarchal education. First, while preaching the reality principle, he ignores the reality of many (perhaps most) human beings.

> A hundred years ago, the child's confrontation with reality began with
> the realization of death, which might come through the death of a sib-
> ling, a friend, or a parent, aunt, uncle, or grandparent, any of which
> was far more likely then than now to be experienced by the young.

Today, in contrast, the death of a child is so rare a misfortune as to be thought nearly unbearable, and increases in the life span have significantly postponed the time at which most children experience the death of an elder. (p. 4)

Silber is not living in inner-city America, nor in rural areas afflicted by pollution-induced childhood cancers, nor in countries where parents disappear or families are blown to bits. Every one of my own quite privileged children has personally known at least two—and in some cases three or four—people who have been murdered. Silber is right to point to television as a medium that distorts reality, one that suggests that people "blown away" later get up and go home. But he is out of touch with the actual world in which children live today.

Moreover, by suggesting that the death of a child a hundred years ago was *not* "nearly unbearable," he shows himself entirely separated from women's reality. He should read *The Exile* (1936), Pearl Buck's biography of her mother, and hear Carie grieve—almost to death—for child after child.

The importance of this discussion lies not in the significance of John Silber's pronouncements. The importance lies in recognizing that this callous death orientation is embedded in traditional education. When we tear education from the existential roots of life—discussing evil only in *Moby Dick*, God only in a survey of world religions, creation only in brief mention of a Big Bang, love only in Romeo and Juliet—we are part of a death orientation. Nothing—including the adolescent spirit—survives intact. When mathematics learning is confined to the polished mathematical products of thinkers who actually lived and struggled with matters they themselves held more important, we are part of a death orientation. Finally, when we suppose, as Silber does and Freud did, that moral life depends on ethical terror, we are part of a death orientation.

Of course death should be discussed, and I'll say more about how we might do this in Chapter 5, but it should not be presented as that which motivates obedience and hard work—and, thus, ensures success. The love that precedes and accompanies birth, the parental love that nurtures and sustains, should be emphasized as the root of moral life (Noddings, 1989; Sagan, 1988). It is this love that literally and metaphorically says "yes" to life. In it moral life appears as a promise of goodness and openness. It wants to enhance moral communion more than it wants to produce moral agency. Love wants to support, not to threaten. It promises to "stay with"—not to separate and to judge. In it, all questions are sacred and real life is not hung up like a shroud in the locker outside classrooms.

I have already mentioned existential questions that can be discussed in analytic geometry and probability. When students encounter truth tables in mathematics, they should hear something of their inventor, Ludwig Wittgenstein. Producing a positivist philosophy to guide science, Wittgenstein at the same time believed that the most important things in life escape science. Said Wittgenstein (1922/1971), "There are, indeed, things that cannot be put into words. They *make themselves manifest*. They are what is mystical" (p. 151; 6.522). Did such thinking influence his life? Well, he gave away the considerable fortune he inherited and spent a significant part of his life in manual labor, sometimes working as a gardener—making manifest something he thought could not be clearly said. Later in life, he chided a fellow philosopher for letting a houseplant die. His point was clear: A moment taken from philosophical analysis to water a plant affirms life—manifests something more than can be said.

One would think, looking at today's high schools and even at educational treatises, that the purpose of life (for teenagers) is to get into a good college and that the meaning of life is entirely bound up in material success. Far too little discussion centers on the dignity of work and the interdependence of people who work in a variety of fields ranging from vegetable growing to law. Children should *not* be taught that education is a means to escape the work of their parents. That same work may or may not be appropriate for them—just as it may or may not have been appropriate or satisfying for their parents. Rather, one purpose of education should be to develop an understanding and appreciation of existence, of life lived fully aware— "wide awake," as Maxine Greene (1978) puts it.

As teachers and students talk to each other about the meaning of life, attention should be given to pessimists—to the "sick souls" as William James called them—as well as to those who take positions of scientific or religious optimism. Often, as James admitted, the sick souls present a more accurate picture of human reality than their sunnier brothers and sisters.

Why do I suggest attention to pessimist thought in high school? Teenagers, by and large, are a gloomy lot. Witness the dreadful lyrics on suicide, murder, and despair that many "enjoy," the continuing self-doubts they experience, and the violent solutions they often fantasize. Just as students who are experimenting with drugs need to know that mind- and soul-enhancing substances have long enticed human beings (they are not the first), so worried teenagers need to know that many intelligent human beings have suffered realistic depression.

They need to know that even successful and usually optimistic persons have suffered periods of intense self-denigration and general revulsion in reaction to the obvious evils of the world. James (1902/1958) quotes Goethe as follows: "I will say nothing against the course of my existence. But at bottom it has been nothing but pain and burden, and I can affirm that during the whole of my 75 years, I have not had four weeks of genuine well-being. It is but the perpetual rolling of a rock that must be raised up again" (p. 119). Martin Luther, with his personal history of enormous success, sometimes looked back on his life as a complete failure. Robert Louis Stevenson commented that "we are not intended to succeed; failure is the fate allotted" (quoted in James, 1902/1958, p. 120). But Stevenson, who, like Goethe and Luther, was *not* a pessimist, went on to say, "Our business is to continue to fail in good spirits" (p. 120).

A study of failure and feelings of failure is perhaps healthier than the total denial of failure that we often urge upon teachers and students. Of course we want students to succeed—but not at everything and, certainly, not at everything equally. And there is surely no need to *mark* them as failures—to expose their shortcomings to the world as a "permanent record." A life-oriented education would assist students in realistic self-evaluation, in seeing both the humor and sadness in failure, and in recognizing that some failures contribute to the discovery of our real talents.

Both believers and unbelievers—intelligent ones—show at least a tinge of pessimism. Sadness, James (1902/1958) reminded us, is central not only in Christianity and Buddhism, but lies also

> at the heart of every merely positivistic, agnostic, or naturalistic scheme of philosophy. Let sanguine healthy-mindedness do its best with its strange power of living in the moment and ignoring and forgetting, still the evil background is really there to be thought of and the skull will grin in at the banquet. (p. 121)

James himself is eloquent enough on the horrors of life to satisfy the gloom of any teenager—perhaps even to bring a smile to young lips. After all, the "infernal cat" playing with "the panting mouse" is also a cuddly pet that has comforted many a child or weary old woman. And the "loathsome existence" of "crocodiles and rattlesnakes and pythons" and other wild beasts clutching their living prey might be described in terms other than "loathsome." Having heard James, students might acknowledge the accuracy of his description but, like James himself, sees its limitations. Even a "loathsome existence" may have its moments of grace and beauty and serve purposes beyond the visible horrors.

How do human beings balance the horror and absurdity so obvious in life with the instinct to live and the longing for happiness? Many, like Thoreau, turn to nature. Indeed a class might need a walk in the park or a rest on the lawn after hearing parts of James's chapter on the sick soul. Why must field trips always be information-gathering expeditions? Why can't they occasionally be soul-saving missions?

Dance is another soul-restorer. Little children, pagans, Hasidim, Sufis, lovers, and priests at the altar all dance to celebrate both the sadness and joy of life. How often do gym teachers talk to their students about dance as a form of spiritual restoration? Do math teachers ever join in the dance? Students should be invited, of course, to reflect on their own dance forms and whether their dancing is restorative or debilitating.

Music, art, poetry, storytelling, and drama are not just modes of cultural transmission. All can contribute to the balance we are discussing here, and all can and have in well-known cases also contributed to imbalance. Students need help in choosing forms that, for them, are genuinely restorative. The search for meaning implies a continual concomitant search for means of restoration.

Finally, students should hear many, many biographical accounts of those who have found consolation and joy in work, dance, the arts, or human love and dedication, and also of those who have found theirs in ritual, prayer, or religious devotion. (The modes are not mutually exclusive, of course.) Even an unbeliever can be moved by the story of John Henry Newman (later Cardinal Newman) suffering "sickness, doubt, and perplexity" on a sea voyage (Butterworth, 1875, p. 215). "With a sky of Italian splendors and dangers above him, and the sea rocking the ship beneath," he wrote:

> Lead, Kindly Light, amid the encircling gloom,
>   Lead Thou me on;
> The night is dark, and I am far from home,
>   Lead Thou me on.
> Keep Thou my feet; I do not ask to see
> The distant scene; one step enough for me.

. . .
So long thy power blest me, sure it still
　　Will lead me on
O'er moor and fen, o'er crag and torrent, till
　　The night is gone,
And with the morn those angel faces smile
Which I have loved long since, and lost awhile.
(quoted in Butterworth, 1875, p. 215)

Thus Newman answers Millay, who was "not resigned."

In closing this chapter, we have to ask whether the suggestions I've made so far are reasonable, practical, feasible. On one level, they clearly are. I've demonstrated what can be done by way of addressing existential questions even in mathematics classes. But, on another level, my recommendations sketch a scenario that defies reality. Why is the scenario so unimaginable as a plan for actual schools? When we look at the possibilities I have outlined and at the real world of schools—when we look wide-awake at the two—we may feel what Emily Dickinson called "zero at the bone." The unimaginableness of my scenario reveals the depravity in which we live and work because, of course, it *is* entirely possible to educate for intelligent belief or unbelief. We just do not care enough—are not alive enough—not wide-awake enough—to do it.

Whether or not we believe often depends on our conception of God, and that is the subject of Chapter 2. Martin Buber (1967) was once asked if he believed in God, and he assured his questioner that he did. But then he heard an inner voice speaking.

"If to believe in God means to be able to talk about him in the third person, then I do not believe in God. If to believe in him means to be able to talk to him, then I believe in God." And after a while, further: "The God who gives Daniel such foreknowledge of this hour of human history, this hour before the 'world war,' that its fixed place in the march of the ages can be foredetermined, is not my God and not God. The God to whom Daniel prays in his suffering is my God and the God of all." (pp. 24-25)

Buber is faithful to his vision when he says that one conception is not his God and another is, but he contradicts himself when he goes on to say that the God of foreknowledge is "not God" and that the God to whom Daniel prays in his suffering *is* God. How easily we fall into describing the indescribable.

CHAPTER 2

The Nature of Gods

Both believers and unbelievers have conceptions of the gods they believe in or disavow. Indeed, some believers lose their faith and join unbelievers because they can no longer subscribe to the vision of deity presented in their traditional religion. What are the options for intelligent belief, and how can they be discussed in school? Whereas most of my examples in Chapter 1 came from mathematics and science, most of the examples in this chapter will be from literature and history.

Polytheism is one religious alternative that is easy to discuss in schools because it is almost never taken seriously. Students are forced to read mythology and many are fascinated by the antics of the gods, but rarely does anyone suggest that polytheism is a logical possibility for today's religious spirit. Dualism is a modification of polytheism (or, sometimes, of monotheism) that posits two great powers—a God of good and one of evil in continual struggle. This, too, is a position accepted by many today. An even greater modification yields one God but many minor powers espousing evil causes. Finally, of course, there is strict monotheism, belief in one God. Even here, we find an array of possibilities. Is the one God personal or impersonal? Male, female, neither, or both? Is God embodied in the universe, or does God stand outside the universe as creator? Is the creator interested in his (her or its) creation? Can one communicate with God? In short, the questions to be considered here center on the nature of gods we believe in.

MONOTHEISM

Most people in today's Western culture are brought up to believe in one God or no God. Their choice is further limited by the nature of the one God as it is described in their family tradition. The choice is bluntly stated by Arthur Gibson (1969) in his interpretive study of seven of Ingmar Bergman's films.

> There is no "new God." There is only the old God more clearly seen, more bravely faced, encountered on man's part with more of the courage displayed by that God himself in creating free creatures. In extremely plastic form, with pre-eminently plastic images, these films reveal the elements of human experience that lead some to conclude to atheism and others to conclude to theism. (p. 157)

We cannot possibly treat all of the difficulties that arise for belief under monotheism. We will not even be able to describe all of its forms, and I would not be qualified to do this in any case. What we, as educators, can and must do is to acquaint students with some of the major conflicts in monotheism, encourage them to ask questions, and explore the realm of spirituality as fully as their needs demand.

The Silence of God

Starting with films such as Bergman's or commentaries on films, or literature, some of the most pressing problems can be identified. Gibson (1969) says that modern atheists do not demand a more up-to-date God or a more sophisticated treatment of religious mythology, although they might appreciate such moves intellectually. Rather, intelligent atheism

> is a result of inspection of the sum total of reality available to modern man. It enunciates at the end of its inspection: I find nowhere the kind or species of reality designated in the past as God, Allah, Yahweh, or even Supreme Creator. (p. 156)

The difficulty for most atheists is that they neither see nor hear any sign of God. It is fair to say here that deists, who neither hear nor see any sign of a personal God, nevertheless acknowledge a Supreme Creator. They take as their evidence the existence of the universe and life itself, but they deny that a Supreme Creator must necessarily have an interest in the individuals living their brief lives within the great creation. In another variation, the supreme creator gives way to creation itself. (This is a response induced by the questions raised in Chapter 1: If God created the universe, who or what created God? And if God created himself or herself, why couldn't the creation create itself?) But these positions do not satisfy spiritual longing. They can at best encourage aesthetic appreciation and awe.

Most people want a God with whom they can communicate, one who cares what happens in their lives.

The absence or silence of God is a frequent theme in poetry. Thomas Hardy, in "The Impercipient," wrote:

> Since heart of mine knows not the ease
> Which they know; since it be
> That He who breathes All's Well to these
> Breathes no All's Well to me,
> My lack might move their sympathies
> And Christian charity!
>
> I am like a gazer who should mark
> An inland company
> Standing upfingered, with, "Hark! hark!
> The glorious distant sea!"
> And feel, "Alas, 'tis but yon dark
> And wind-swept pine to me!"
>
> Yet I would bear my shortcomings
> With meet tranquillity,
> But for the charge that blessed things
> I'd liefer not have be.
> O, doth a bird deprived of wings
> Go earth-bound wilfully!

Robert Frost's well-known poem, "Stopping by Woods on a Snowy Evening," is another that suggests the absence of God and a longing to make contact with the architect of nature: "Whose woods these are, I think I know. His house is in the village though . . ." These words are widely interpreted as a reference to the absent God.

Bergman's films also convey the silence of God. In his interpretations, Gibson blames the Bergman characters for failing to see or hear God or for expecting a form of communication in which God does not engage. This kind of argument is persuasive for many theists who report perceiving God in the silences. Consider one of the most terrible incidents in *The Seventh Seal*. A young woman, Tyan, has enlivened her humdrum life through imaginative communication with the Devil. She hears something others do not hear although they acknowledge the reality of her companion. When she is burned at the stake—expecting rescue right up to the moment of excruciating pain—there is no response from the Devil to her cries. What if she had called on God? Here the problem of silence becomes dramatic.

Surely the physical result would have been exactly the same. The compassionate, humanistic squire, Jons, sees this and engages his knight in this revealing dialogue.

> Jons: What does she see? Can you tell?
> Knight: (shakes his head): She feels no more pain.
> Jons: You don't answer my question. Who watches over that child? Is it the angels, or God, or the Devil, or only emptiness? Emptiness, my lord!
> Knight: This cannot be.
> Jons: Look at her eyes, my lord. Her poor brain has just made a discovery. Emptiness under the moon.
> Knight: No.
> Jons: We stand powerless, our arms hanging at our sides, because we see what she sees, and our terror and hers are the same. (An outburst) That poor little girl. I can't stand it, I can't stand it . . . (quoted in Gibson, 1969, p. 21)

Believers and unbelievers part company when one group sees or hears what the other group perceives as silence. But sometimes believers give up their belief because the nature of the God pressed on them is too horrible. In the medieval setting of *The Seventh Seal*, authorities would probably have insisted that Tyan could have been safe in heaven had she repented and called upon the true God. Keeping faith with the Devil until the end, she was doomed and damned. This is too much for compassionate onlookers like Jons, and they become unbelievers. If they could believe that she would be all right no matter what in the hands of a compassionate God (who could, after all, understand teenage foolishness), they might maintain a form of belief. But would such a God allow burning the misguided at the stake? And, then, what would be the point of so much elaborate courting of God if all were cordially received no matter what they believed? As one youngster said to another in *The Cardinal*, "If it's true like he [the priest] says—that any old hard-shell Baptist can get into heaven—what's the use of going to all this trouble to be a Catholic?" (Robinson, 1952, p. 88).

It seems clear that we cannot settle the matter of God's presence or absence by looking at cases where some hear and others experience silence. Compassionate humanists say there is just one conclusion we can properly draw from such events: We must be present to each other, reject cruelty, and respond to suffering with gentle hands. Many theists agree that we should behave just as the humanist recommends but that this is what God wants and that, when we respond with compassion, we are participating in God's love (McNeill, Morrison, & Nouwen, 1983). Harry Emerson Fosdick (1961) says this of God:

> He is in his greatness incomprehensible, but he has a near end. Where integrity and justice are; where goodness, truth, and beauty are; where right triumphs over wrong, light dispels darkness and good-will conquers hate, there is God. As Tolstoi says, "Where love is, there is God also." . . . There are social movements whose pillar of cloud by day and of fire by night are justice for the oppressed, liberation for the enslaved, equality of opportunity, the conquest of racial discrimination, the abolition of war. That is the near end of God. (p. 90)

The difficulty raised by these lovely attributions (and Christian literature is filled with them) is that everything good that is achieved or happens is attributed to God. Students should appreciate the power of the message—a call to service and commitment—but they should also be urged to examine the logic. If we could point to a visible entity and say, "Here is God; expect only good," we would have an airtight case. But to say, "Here is good; God must be here," rings hollow to unbelievers. The silence in moments of great need is decisive.

The problem of silence is greater for monotheism than for polytheism. This is not a necessary fact but a contingent one. Monotheism in the Christian tradition insists that God is all-good, all-powerful, and all-knowing. Polytheisms usually grant that gods are partly good, partly evil, powerful but not omnipotent, knowing but capable of being deceived. Both good and evil find their roots in divine action. Christians have to find God in bright spots and silver linings. Even Jews, whose tradition recognizes the raging side of God more fully, have difficulty reconciling events like the Holocaust with their understanding of God. I'll say more about the problem of evil a bit later.

Religious Intolerance and Spiritual Progress

The insistence on a perfect, one-and-only God also leads to religious intolerance. This is not to say that polytheistic societies are peaceable either internally or externally, but they are not usually characterized by the sense of superiority and moral urgency that marks monotheism. Writing of the Egyptian king Amenhotep IV, Freud (1939) remarked:

> This king undertook to force upon his subjects a new religion, one contrary to their ancient traditions and to all their familiar habits. It was a strict monotheism, the first attempt of its kind in the history of the world, as far as we know; and religious intolerance, which was foreign to antiquity before this and for long after, was inevitably born with the belief in one God. (p. 21)

This brings us to a problem that cannot be explored thoroughly in schools but should at least be raised. Does monotheism represent spiritual progress and, if so, in what sense? Students may respond initially by pointing to the rejection of superstition. We no longer believe, for example, that if a volcano erupts, the volcano-God must be appeased. We no longer sacrifice human beings in the effort at appeasement. (Are there no superstitions, then, in contemporary monotheism? What *is* a superstition?) Noting the rejection of human sacrifice, students may point to the great ethical contributions of monotheism. Here we have deity as lawgiver, not capricious wielder of power. (What are these laws? How have they contributed to community life? Are they equally protective of all parties? Has their revision come from within religion or has it been pressed from outside?) As students recognize the fact that religious ethics have not protected all people equally, they may be led to question whether some people have suffered spiritual as well as political deprivation under the familiar forms of monotheism. (How do women feel about the image of God as father? How do colonial peoples feel about the loss of their ancestral gods?) Finally, students should be encouraged to circle back and ask what we mean by progress in general. The aim here is not to destroy belief or simply to debunk religion but to induce both skepticism and genuine appreciation (Noddings, 1992). An exploration of progress—technological, spiritual, medical, political, and ethical— would make a wonderful interdisciplinary unit, one in which science, English, and social studies teachers could collaborate.

The topic of spiritual progress was triggered by Freud's comments on monotheism and religious intolerance. This is an extremely important topic for students to consider, and its usual treatment in schools is superficial and often misleading. We are afraid to challenge the real bigotry and nonsense in many religions, and we therefore treat cowardly silence as tolerance. But there is dreadful bigotry in all forms of fundamentalism and plenty of nonsense in almost every institutional form of religion. Students need to read and criticize extreme and oppositional accounts of events and lives; they need opportunities to ferret out the bits of truth in chauvinistic speeches and the chunks of untruth in glowing stories of religious heroes. To ignore either is to promote religious intolerance through ignorance and, worse, self-righteousness.

Consider an example. Many Western young people today are drawn to Eastern religions. We educators should not try to immunize them against this attraction, nor should we promote it thoughtlessly. Critics of intellectuals often accuse us of promoting everything foreign, different, and exotic while denigrating everything homegrown, traditional, and familiar. There is a grain of truth in this accusation even when it is embedded in exaggeration and inaccuracy. Suppose we started a unit of study with the film *Gandhi*. (Because of the length of the film, we might have to use clips or a written account, but it would be better to show the whole film.) From the film, students get a sense of Gandhi as a civic and spiritual hero. They may also find attractive features in Hinduism.

Now let's have them read Richard Grenier's (1983) *The Gandhi Nobody Knows*. This is a scathing account of Gandhi's inconsistency, his callous treatment of those close to him, his obsession with defecation, and his psychological violence. Grenier's is not a balanced treatment, and it also paints a nasty picture of Hinduism. Students should be encouraged to sort through the two presentations. Is the film a bold, political, paid advertisement for India, as Grenier insists? Are there signs of religious intolerance in Grenier's book? *Do* we have something to be proud of in the American religious tradition that Grenier holds up as superior to Hinduism? Why does Grenier devote so much space to Gandhi's interest in bowel movements and the Hindu practice of drinking urine? What effect does that emphasis have on Western readers? Do Hindus believe in God? In exploring these questions, teachers should be ready to refer students to a host of sources where they can learn more about religious asceticism, bodily humiliation, deism and other views of God as creative force, nonviolence, chastity, rituals, and especially the power of particular language and topics with selected populations. Students might also be led to read other, more balanced biographies of Gandhi such as Robert Payne's (1969) *The Life and Death of Mahatma Gandhi*. The aim throughout is to promote critical and appreciative intelligence, to develop self and group understanding, to learn how to investigate and make connections.

I would not leave a unit on Gandhi without discussing his humanism quite thoroughly. Should Christians, Jews, and Moslems be critical because he used more than one name for God or, perhaps, even believed in a multitude of gods? Because, in extremis, he called on Rama? Consider what he sought to teach us.

In Gandhi's nonviolent campaigns the enemy was seen as a mirror of aspects of oneself that one needed to confront and absorb rather than merely reject. The enemy is, in a strange way, one's collaborator against social evil. The nonviolent warrior goes into battle against injustice *with* his Jungian shadow, not against it. The goal is not to eliminate others but to transform them into friends. And this is no mere trick to lead them to compromise their principles; for Gandhi, one must be willing to change oneself, to give in to reason, to respond to the kindnesses of others, to compromise and seek mutuality, and to suffer out the consequences of living for truths someone else denies or cannot see. (Inchausti, 1991, p. 21)

Human Dependence on God

So far I have mentioned three major problems for monotheistic believers: the apparent silence of God, religious intolerance (about which much more will be said in Chapter 3), and the notion of spiritual progress. A balanced treatment must include both the great contributions and the dreadful harms of monotheism. Most important of all, the discussion must encourage curiosity and reflective thought.

Having said that, another problem arises, and this problem is shared by all religions to some degree. From the days of the early Greeks, people have been warned that they are dependent on gods. In many of the Greek tragedies, heroes are toppled by unresolvable conflicts between two sets of values—one usually anchored in human love and desire, the other in the will of the gods. Often one of the gods seems to show his or her power by bringing a hero down. Euripedes shows in *Hecuba* what can happen to a person of good character who depends on humanly constructed ethics for guidance. (See Nussbaum, 1986, for a lively account connecting the tragedies to Aristotle's thought.) The story yields at least two distinct messages: First, humans must acknowledge their dependence on the gods, for human values are necessarily fragile; second, in direct opposition, humans must accept the risks that accompany complete responsibility for the creation and maintenance of value. All religions have adopted the first, insisting that no matter how fine the values, they will prove unstable if not backed by the gods; that is, we are called to acknowledge that we need a source of value stronger and firmer than ourselves. Daring to think otherwise, we commit the sin of pride.

The message of dependence and the need for submission is especially strong in Christianity. Again and again, thinking adults are called upon to be "as little children," accepting the message of God as expressed in the gospel. R. C. Zaehner (1974), in *Our Savage God*, goes so far as to title one of his chapters "Islam." The chapter has nothing whatever to do with Muslim religion. The word *Islam* means submission, and Zaehner sees submission as central to Christian faith. The difficulty, of course, is that disagreements arise over the meanings of submission, and considerable intellectual sophistication is required to debate the issues. Christian practice differs widely here. In some denominations, intellectual debate is encouraged in matters of practical interpretation but not on basic doctrines of faith; in others, everything is prescribed, and questioning is itself a sin; and in a few, even doctrines of faith can be debated. But submission itself cannot be challenged. Gibson (1969), in his commentary on Bergman's *Persona*, describes the moment of submission.

> This moment is the supreme approach to a perfect God–man communication. Man is ready for only a moment, to be sure, but for a supremely vital moment, to accept and adopt the only relational position proper to him or fruitful for him, utterly exposed to the power of God. (p. 143)

But this does not mean that God will tell us what to do or that he will communicate with us in intelligible human signs. Gibson faults Bergman's characters repeatedly for making this assumption. Gibson says that God cannot be approached as "the answerer of questions and gratifier of human curiosity" or as the "satisfier of human needs" (p. 168). Rather God calls for "a simultaneous total passivity and courageous activity." Man must accept his creaturely status and yet shoulder moral responsibility—"must fare forward to the good fight, never certain of the outcome, *because he must contribute to that outcome*" (p. 167).

Here we come to the heart of a difficulty to be discussed more completely in Chapter 3. The position recommended by Gibson can lead to horrendous conclusions. Submitting entirely to authority, one either does what that authority says to do, or—in the silence of that authority—one acts vigorously on the assumption that submission itself somehow justifies or supports the action. In Gibson's theology, God is primarily creator; he does not give direct commands. This can be ethically dangerous. As Ricoeur (1969) remarks, "The clearer God becomes as legislator, the more obscure he becomes as creator," and vice versa (p. 315). Gibson, of course, refers us to the life of Christ for ethical guidance, but—living in different times, in different bodies, in different cultures—his life, too, must be interpreted, and again the silence of God, the creator, engulfs us.

In contrast, Judaism has always put tremendous emphasis on

God as legislator. Recognizing God as creator, Abraham Neuman (1961) goes on to write of the early Hebrew religion:

> He placed the forces of nature at the command of man, if man would but heed the commands of God. The commands lie in the practice of justice, righteousness, morality, and holiness. Man's abiding by these laws renders his life godly and secure. Virtue is promptly rewarded. Sin meets with quick retribution. (p. 14)

This is early Judaism. When it became clear that virtue is not always rewarded and sin not always met with retribution in this life, interest in immortality increased, for justice must be done in the next life. But then how can we be sure what is virtue and what sin? The role of ritual is enormously important in Jewish life because it connects people to the general commands of God, reminds them that the commands are there to give backbone to their decisions, and ties them to each other in community. But interpretation is still crucial, and the silence and absence of God are problems for Jewish thinkers too (Wiesel, 1960).

If the nature of God with respect to metaphysical questions is fraught with ambiguities, so is God as legislator. Jewish thought concentrates on these difficulties. Martin Buber struggled with many biblical passages. Looking to God as giver of ethics, he particularly suffered over passages that suggest a vengeful and evil streak in God. Consider I Samuel, chapter 15. Here Samuel castigates Saul for leaving Agag, king of the Amalekites, alive. (All the others had been killed.) Samuel insists that obedience to God means to kill all. When Agag is brought before Samuel, he implicitly pleads for his life, saying, "Surely the bitterness of death is past" (15:32). Samuel's response is, " 'As the sword hath made women childless, so shall thy mother be childless among women.' And Samuel hewed Agag in pieces before the Lord" (15:33). Buber could not accept a God who would give such an order, and he decided that Samuel must have misunderstood God (Friedman, 1991). When we concentrate on God as lawgiver, this is the kind of struggle we face. Has God grown better over time? Have we learned better how to listen and interpret? Should we accept and worship a cruel, erratic, and jealous God? Or should we simply acknowledge that we cannot understand and simply submit?

The demand for submission and childlike acceptance raises special problems for educators. How do we encourage students to ask what A. N. Wilson (1991) calls "awkward questions" about religion if their own religion discourages a critical approach? There is no easy answer to this. I think we have to encourage the questions but in a sensitive and humane way that not only protects uncritical believers from ridicule but also encourages deeper appreciation and understanding in unbelievers. Education is hardly worthy of its name if it allows nonsense to go unchallenged, but it is also unworthy if it produces insensitive and spiritually illiterate skeptics.

Another feature of human dependence on gods should be mentioned. Not only must humans depend on gods for ethical guidance, but also humans are at the mercy of gods for good or ill fortune. This is not a problem for polytheism or, even, for deterministic monotheism because both accept as fact that gods visit real or apparent evils on humans. But it is a great problem for those forms of monotheism insisting on an all-good God. Increasingly, this position is taken in both Christian and Jewish teaching. McNeill, Morrison, and Nouwen (1983) write:

> We are often tempted to "explain" suffering in terms of "the will of God." Not only can this evoke anger and frustration, but it is also false. "God's will" is not a label that can be put on unhappy situations. God wants to bring joy not pain, peace not war, healing not suffering. Therefore, instead of declaring anything and everything to be the will of God, we must be willing to ask ourselves where in the midst of our pains and sufferings we can discern the loving presence of God. (p. 40)

To intelligent believers, this view represents spiritual progress. Why, after all, should we worship a God who is poorer than the best humans in compassion and ethicality? But the intelligent unbeliever has a continuing problem. How do we know that God wants to bring joy, peace, and healing? Given the evidence in our empirical world and, especially, the biblical record, what justifies us in choosing only the messages of love?

The Problem of Evil

These questions belong to the problem of evil, one that has kept theologians busy for centuries. The basic question is this: How can we explain the presence of evil in a world created and run by a God who is all-good, all-knowing, and all-powerful? In Christian theodicy, the problem amounts to rescuing God from complicity in evil. Traditional theodicies trace the origin of evil to the human inclination to turn away from God and toward things of this world. Augustinian theodicy regards the result as inevitable and just. For

Augustine, suffering in life and suffering in hell are necessary in a perfect universe, because moral evil must be balanced by retribution. Augustine and many philosophers and theologians following him— even the great mathematician Leibniz—accepted "the wisdom of God's decision to allow most human souls to suffer eternal damnation" (Noddings, 1989, p. 19). A happier perspective in traditional theodicy saw the Fall (which for Augustine justified all that followed) as a "necessary sin and a happy fault." In this view, the evil we suffer is still justified but now it is aimed at our own perfection. After expulsion from Eden, we were forced to seek and learn, to develop both intellectually and morally (Hick, 1966). In the traditional theodicies, we are compelled to regard apparent evil as either no evil at all (a figment of our human shortsightedness) or required for our own good in the long run. The Augustinian view has been especially damaging. Ricoeur (1969) comments:

> The harm that has been done to souls, during the centuries of Christianity, first by literal interpretation of the story of Adam, and then by confusion of this myth, treated as history, with later speculations, principally Augustinian, about original sin, will never be adequately told. (p. 239)

Even today, many writers whose work is enormously popular have taken the traditional view of suffering. C. S. Lewis (1976), for example, tried to explain his wife's agony with cancer this way.

> But is it credible that such extremities of torture should be necessary for us? Well, take your choice. The tortures occur. If they are unnecessary, then there is no God or a bad one. If there is a good God, then these tortures are necessary. For no even moderately good Being could possibly inflict or permit them if they weren't. (p. 50)

The idea that life is a form of soul-making is still held by many.

There are, however, alternatives. Process theology offers at least two alternatives. One is to attribute both good and evil to God as the early Hebrews did and many Jews do even today; the other is to relax the insistence on God's omnipotence. In particular, we can argue that God cannot logically give his creatures free will and, at the same time, protect them from all harm. Some things, lots of things, just happen, as Kushner (1981) says in *When Bad Things Happen to Good People*. God cannot control everything. Kushner urges us to consider a response, rather than an explanation, to the question why bad things happen to good people. He says:

> The response would be Job's response in MacLeish's version of the
> biblical story—to forgive the world for not being perfect, to forgive God
> for not making a better world, to reach out to the people around us,
> and to go on living despite it all. (p. 147)

From this perspective, one can still get help from God in times
of pain and tragedy but that help does not come in the form of
answers to the question, "Why?" nor in release from tragedy. It
gives us strength to live and to do better with each other. Why, then,
asks the thoughtful unbeliever, can't we just do this from the start?
Why bother with God at all if his only answer is to turn to each
other? Because, respond believers, God is real and we need the
strength God gives us to accomplish the task. Further, God supplies
the center of community and the focus of ritual, both of which bind
us to each other. Struggling with the problem of evil, intelligent believers and unbelievers are, at one and the same time, closer to each
other and farther apart than on any other issues.

The other alternative in process theology is to give up the assumption that God is all-good. This alternative is less attractive to
today's spirit than the one that gives up omnipotence, but it has an
obvious history in biblical record. There is no logically convincing
way to make the God of the Pentateuch all-good. He is Zaehner's
Savage God—a powerful, jealous, and irrational bully. Carl Jung
(1973) has presented a fascinating account of God's own moral
growth in *Answer to Job*. Basically, Jung declares that the male God
needs the addition of Sophia, feminine wisdom, to manage his omniscience. He also recommends the integration of God's dark side into
humankind's vision of deity. Because people consciously or uncon-
sciously imitate the deity they envision, these integrations would
contribute greatly to self-understanding. I'll say a bit more about
Jung's analysis in the section on polytheism and again in Chapter 4
on feminism and religion.

In this brief discussion of monotheism, I have identified several
problems that high school students should be aware of: the silence of
God, the notion of spiritual progress, the religious intolerance associated with monotheism, the demand for submission, and the
problem of evil. More will be said about God as lawgiver in Chapter
7 on ethics. In addition, there are basic questions students should be
encouraged to ask themselves, but they should not be forced to discuss them publicly. Rather, they should hear other voices exploring
them: Must the God I worship be all-powerful, all-good, and all-
knowing? Is there a political agenda connected with the description

of a father-God as perfect? How would I feel about a well-meaning but imperfect God? How would I feel about a mother-God?

We should not expect teachers to handle these problems in sophisticated theological or philosophical ways. Such an expectation is unrealistic, and if by some miracle it were met, the resulting experience could be ruinous. All the vitality might be drained from the experience. Both students and teachers should explore these problems as deeply as they need to for individual and group self-understanding. One could begin the exploration with films, literature, and commentaries. Students should also have an opportunity to read the book of Job, surely one of the greatest literary achievements of all time. They could also read Kushner's interpretation and, with the help of a commentary, teachers could tell them something of Jung's interpretation and what it means for spiritual progress.

DUALISM

Dualisms posit good and evil powers warring in the cosmos. One of the best known such views is found in Zoroastrianism where Ahura Mazda and Ahriman are in a perpetual contest. As a modification of polytheism, dualism allows the worship (or at least appeasement) of both powers. As a modification of monotheism, dualism relieves God of responsibility for evil and calls on humans to help God in the war for good. Many Christian theologies, including the Roman Catholic, regard dualism as a heresy because it denies the omnipotence of God. Also, as Augustine saw so clearly, in locating evil at the level of deity, it allows people to shrug off the evil they themselves invent. But dualism has its attractive side. Augustine went too far in blaming human beings for the world's suffering, and the thought that evil is at least in part a state that precedes our existence helps us to detach evil from sin.

Forms of dualism are found today in protestant sects. The devil is recognized as a real power in a war for souls. Many people know the work of psychiatrist M. Scott Peck. Peck (1983) accepts dualism and says:

> According to this model, humanity (and perhaps the entire universe) is locked in a titanic struggle between the forces of good and evil, between God and the devil. The battleground of this struggle is the individual human soul. The only question of ultimate significance is whether the individual soul will be won to God or won to the devil. (p. 37)

Pacts with the devil are recognized in both monotheism and dualism, but only in dualism is the cosmic end result in question. Peck (1983) describes what he sees at stake in a case that arose in his psychiatric practice.

> By establishing through this pact a relationship with the devil, George had placed his soul in the greatest jeopardy known to man. It was clearly the critical point of his life. And possibly the fate of all humanity turned upon his decision. Choirs of angels and armies of demons were watching him, hanging on his every thought, praying continually for one outcome or the other. (pp. 37–38)

This is a prominent position in many forms of fundamentalism. It is important to discuss because perhaps more than half the U.S. population today believes in the devil—not just as an impersonal force for evil, as the deists might see God as creator—but as a personal entity who can influence lives. So many well-educated people ridicule this view that it rarely gets any sort of hearing in educational settings. In Scott Peck, we have a highly educated, thoughtful, and compassionate professional who believes that human beings can communicate with both God and the devil.

A second reason for mentioning dualism is that it solves a huge theological problem. Positing an evil power in direct opposition to God relieves God of responsibility for evil. All evil comes from the evil power; all good from God. Process theology, mentioned earlier, makes a sophisticated move in this direction. It preserves monotheism but gives up *monism*. It posits a creative power independent of God, one whose chaotic creations are shaped and ordered by God. This power is not a being, so God is still the one and only supreme being, but the creative power is distributed throughout the universe, and God does not have unilateral control over the entities in which power resides. David Griffin (1991) writes:

> It *is* pluralism, nevertheless, in the sense that there has always been and always will be a plurality of individuals. Our world was created not out of *absolute nothingness*—as if God alone existed once upon a time, or "before time"—but out of a chaos of finite events. (p. 23)

The demonic (devilish, satanic) thus develops right along with goodness because wherever true power exists there is the capacity for good or ill use of it. In this scheme, the absolute goodness of God is clearly essential. God, out of perfect goodness, resists exercising the capacity for evil.

A third reason for discussing dualism is that the theme of power derived from alliances with the devil is a prominent one in literature. Blake, Goethe, and Nietzsche all suggested that human beings could become more powerful and *better* by understanding and working with their devils. As William Barrett (1962) put it:

> Like Blake before him Goethe knew full well the ambiguous power contained in the traditional symbol of the Devil. Nietzsche's immoralism, though stated much more violently, consisted in not much more than the elaboration of Goethe's point: Man must incorporate his devil or, as he put it, man must become better and more evil; the tree that would grow taller must send its roots down deeper. (p. 190)

All three—Blake, Goethe, Nietzsche—seriously entertained the possibility that human beings can become better by accepting the fact that evil must be done to acquire the power required to do good. Only the very strong dare such an alliance with dark forces, and through initial strength and the alliance itself, one becomes still stronger and more powerful. Such powerful people can then act so as to accomplish significant good. What an intriguing and dangerous course of thought!

Now, should we share such difficult, detailed reasoning with high school students? I'm not sure. Once in a while, at least, we should, because we want them to have some sense of the intricacies of theology. (Clearly, most of them will rarely hear any of this from a pulpit.) Whether this is an appropriate topic through which to promote such appreciation is a question I prefer to leave open. Perhaps the most important information for students in this discussion is that in strict monotheism something has to give. Either we move in Jung's direction and integrate evil into the deity itself or we acknowledge dualism or pluralism. The latter seems mathematically right, but the former may give us a morality of evil that could help us to manage our own lives better. To acknowledge both good and evil in our parents, our nation, our religion, our God, and ourselves may be a healthy move psychologically as well as intellectually.

POLYTHEISM

Polytheism, familiar to high school students through Greek, Roman, and Norse myths, is usually associated with superstition, primitive thinking, and paganism. Even when the sophistication of polytheistic thought is acknowledged, a temptation remains to regard strict monotheism as "spiritual progress" (Freud, 1939). Monotheism has indeed produced a form of academic progress marked by huge libraries of speculation on the existence and nature of the one God and what that oneness means for a host of other existential problems, but such speculation—even at its abstract best—does not necessarily represent *spiritual* progress.

There is something direct and attractive in Greek polytheism. As Hazel Barnes (1974) notes, the gods are anthropomorphic but also "personifications of forces in Nature" (p. 100). Thus the world is seen and described in terms of spirit, and the gods are as variable and vexing as human beings. Further, the gods are often interested in human affairs; they take sides and act as guides and champions. Best of all—from a logical point of view—the gods are sources of both good and evil, and so there is no need for an elaborate theodicy. On this, Barnes quotes Nietzsche, who said that the Greek gods "justified human life by living it themselves—the only satisfactory theodicy ever invented" (p. 97; Nietzsche, 1956, p. 30).

William James (1902/1958) saw clearly the advantage of pluralism in theodicy. Acknowledging that a solution might yet be found to the problem of evil in strict monotheistic thought, he wrote:

> The only *obvious* escape from paradox here is to cut loose from the monistic assumption altogether, and to allow the world to have existed from its origin in pluralistic form, as an aggregate or collection of higher and lower things and principles, rather than an absolutely unitary fact. (p. 115)

James (1902/1958) thought that pluralism—some form of polytheism—was humanly as well as logically satisfying. Here is how he put it.

> [The] practical needs and experiences of religion seem to me sufficiently met by the belief that beyond each man and in a fashion continuous with him there exists a larger power which is friendly to him and to his ideals. All that the facts require is that the power should be both other and larger than our conscious selves. Anything larger will do. It need not be infinite, it need not be solitary. It might conceivably even be only a larger and more godlike self, of which the present self would then be but the mutilated expression, and the universe might conceivably be a collection of such selves . . . with no absolute unity realized in it at all. Thus would a sort of polytheism return upon us. (p. 396)

James notes the usual monistic objection to polytheism—that "unless there be one all-inclusive God, our guarantee of security is left imperfect" (p. 396). But just as he is willing to accept chance and randomness in the physical universe, James thinks most of human-kind is willing to settle for a "*chance* of salvation." Although James did not follow up as he promised on these questions, other thinkers certainly might. What is conceivably lost if we are at the mercy of different gods—some good and conscientious, some capricious—might be made up in human ethical life.

Whether or not we find polytheism spiritually satisfying, from a contemporary point of view, it should be seen as eminently logical. We noted in Chapter 1 that, mathematically, the universe is surely a "many"—not a "One" (Rucker, 1982), and, logically, we could even be poly*deists*. We could believe, that is, that a whole meta-universe of gods exists, that it created the sensible universe in which we live, and that it has no concern whatever with our lives as individuals. Students of computer science would surely find a discussion of this possibility intriguing (Hofstadter, 1979, 1985).

An advocate of polytheism might argue this way. Why posit one lonely God? Why not a whole world of gods? Maybe they do watch over us, but perhaps—like human parents—some are more loving, more intelligent, more conscientious than others. This possibility does, as James noted, shake our security. But it should also arouse our compassion. Just as we reach out to neglected children, we might reach out to those neglected by their gods. We might even plead with our God to intervene with the wayward gods.

Besides its logical strengths, which are considerable, polytheism allows each person or group to find its own God or family of gods. Religious intolerance is most often, as we have seen, a product of monotheism. If people were free to explore polytheism deeply, we might find real spiritual progress—that is, an enhanced capacity for all individuals to make meaningful connection to the spiritual realm.

Perhaps the easiest access to contemporary polytheistic thought is found in feminist literature, and I'll say more about this in Chapter 4 on religion and feminism. Here we may simply observe that the establishment of one God—a move that is advertised as inclusive—almost always accelerates exclusion. The "only God" is described in terms favorable to the group that conceives it, and others must worship the strange God or suffer the consequences. For women, both the Jewish and Christian male gods have long symbolized subordination and powerlessness (Daly, 1974). David Kinsley (1989) also notes the strong masculine bias in Jewish and Christian traditions.

> No matter how emphatically one may insist that in this tradition God is not really a person to whom sexual identity may be ascribed, the Judeo-Christian conception of the divine is very strongly compromised in the direction of male imagery and roles. Like it or not, the Judeo-Christian deity for centuries has been imagined as a male person, been assigned male roles, and been steadfastly referred to as "he," "father," and "king." (p. 262)

To conceptualize and describe the gods with whom we communicate is a power that women now want to recapture (Stone, 1976). One need not, of course, insist on polytheism as the only path to religious freedom, and discussion should certainly include the cruelties of historical polytheism, but students should have the opportunity to explore its possibilities.

In the past, we have exposed all our students to mythology as a form of literature. Without this exposure, they would be unable to understand the content of much art, music, drama, and literature, and so the usual rationale for the inclusion of mythology is intellectual. We have rarely treated the spiritual dimension of myths seriously. This, too, I will say more about in Chapter 4, but two elements should be discussed here. First, polytheistic myths may contribute to self-understanding through the study of archetypes; second, a pluralistic conception of deity facilitates a tragic view of life and may thus contribute to self-understanding at the group level. As myths are studied, some Jungian psychology can be introduced. One does not have to accept the concept of archetype exactly as Jung defined it in order to find it useful. Discussion can focus on the psychic forces that seem to operate in all of us. Of these Jung (1969) says:

> These reach down, or up, to quite other levels than so-called common sense would suspect. As *a priori* conditions of all psychic events, they are endued with a dignity which has found immemorial expression in godlike figures. (p. 188)

For Jung, God is a psychic reality; that is, God lives in the collective unconscious, and images of God reflect both the archetypal force and the cultural life in which they are produced. This accounts for the re-emergence of certain types in myth and literature down through the ages: powerful fathers, heroes, godmothers, innocent maidens, witches, ogres, eldest and youngest brothers. Animals and natural phenomena take on symbolic meaning, and themes such as the journey of the hero appear again and again.

If the Jungians are right, the move to monotheism may not be a sign of spiritual progress. It may only be a reflection of intellectual longing and the desire for political power. In it, many elements of the psyche are lost or coagulated in an unhealthy way. What dominates the description of God is the set of ideals found in the superordinate group. It is usually held in Judaism and Christianity that "man" was created in the image of God. But, as Voltaire said, "If God created us in his own image, we have more than reciprocated." The description deliberately omits the shadow side from its conception. Because men have had the power to do so, their conception also leaves out the female, ascribing instead a few feminine traits to an essentially male God.

A careful study of polytheism—from both literary and logical perspectives—shows that developmental tasks and psychic longings are better and more inclusively described than they are in monotheism. Women and others relatively powerless can find images, models, and stories relevant to their own experience. This is not to say, of course, that a return to historical polytheism would advance the cause of women and minorities! It is hard to imagine a more oppressed condition than that of women in classical Athens. But an open reading of polytheistic thought yields insight for individual development. We begin to see what is left out in monotheism.

Another advantage of polytheism is that it relieves humankind of the entire burden of guilt for evil. The polytheistic (or dualistic) conception of deity locates both good and evil in gods. Evil, thus, precedes human existence and is part of the universe into which we are born. Human beings make choices, of course, and sometimes they deliberately or carelessly make evil choices, but from this perspective, evil is not *introduced* by human choice. It is part chosen and part inherited. Ricoeur (1969) says that, from this view, "evil does not begin because it is always already there in some fashion; it is choice *and* heritage" (p. 300). Sometimes we are faced with choices that make evil inevitable, and sometimes we are overwhelmed by ill fortune and cannot invoke our best selves. From a female perspective on ethics, recognition that we are not entirely in control of our own ethical destinies means not that we should depend on a particular prescription from gods but that we should give more help and support to each other (Noddings, 1984). Thinking about a community of

gods with conflicting interests, varying capacities, and different ideals leads us to search either for a supreme God who will bring order
and security to the community or for a process of human interaction
that will achieve the same goals, even if, perhaps, far less perfectly.
Acknowledging a tragic view of life, we can have some sympathy
not only for the inexplicable evils that befall us but even for those we
commit. Without condoning moral evil, we can strive to understand
the circumstances in which it occurs and help to eliminate or avoid
the conditions that give rise to it.

Such an attitude is clearly possible, of course, in monotheistic
thought. We find it often in Jewish thought, in Christian writers
like Unamuno, in philosophers like James, in dramatists like Arthur
Miller, and in poets like Hardy and Frost. A balanced presentation
takes care to show the commonalities as well as the unique features
of monotheism and polytheism.

Contemporary polytheistic thought is also revealed in an increased interest in nature religion. One of the most beautiful and
powerful forms of nature religion is found in American Indian traditions. Amerindian practices can be studied as part of multicultural
education, and, further, the stress on ecological harmony should appeal to many young people who are deeply concerned with the health
of the environment. Catherine Albanese (1991) writes:

> What we, today, would call an ecological perspective came, for the most
> part, easily—if unselfconsciously—among traditional tribal peoples.
> Typically, one apologized to the guardian spirit of an animal or plant
> species for taking the life of the hunted animal or gathered vegetable
> crop. One paid attention, ceremonially, to the cardinal directions, ori-
> enting existence literally by placing oneself in space with reference to all
> its beings and powers. (pp. 23–24)

Among tribal peoples deities were found in "sun, moon, fire,
water, snow, earth, deer, and bear. . . . There were deities of the
four directions, and a woman's god, a children's god, and a house
God as well" (Albanese, 1991, p. 29). For Native Americans in colonial days, the world was a world of spirit. Resisting conversion to
Christianity, one Amerindian asked the missionary, John Eliot,
"Why have not beasts a soul as man hath, seeing they have love,
anger, etc., as man hath?" (Albanese, 1991, p. 30).

New Age thinking shares some beliefs with Native American
thought, but it is often undisciplined. It is parodied in *Doonesbury*

and assailed in critical articles. People are drawn to it by its openness, its interest in nature, and its lack of prescriptive certainty. Consciousness and attitude are primary; action is secondary. Each person must find an acceptable mode of action, and there is assurance that—with the right consciousness—the mode of action, too, will be right. The emphasis on spiritual rather than material life is attractive to many who feel that traditional religions are creatures of the materialistic, political world. But critics point rightly to the lack of action as a weakness, as a form of escape from the world's real problems—not as a solution. Further, New Age criticism of traditional religion is often superficial; it lacks the intelligence we are trying to encourage.

. What do high school students need to know here? First, perhaps, they should learn that spiritual longing is universal and that mystical experience has always been sought and often claimed in convincing accounts. One need not abandon Christianity, Judaism, or Islam to explore mysticism, and students can be directed to sources within the traditional religions. Second, they should learn that all religions demand study and discipline. One can pick up gimmicks from Eastern religion—go about chanting "Om" or whatever—but this hardly counts as practicing a religion or even respecting its practice. It takes considerable study to perform Amerindian rituals properly. To be an intelligent believer one needs to know the weak points as well as the strong points of a religion, the insights and the nonsense, the political and the spiritual. Third, students should come to understand that they can be attracted to a movement by key words. Today's popular attractions include ecology, peace, and harmony. Beautiful as these concepts may be, we need to know what a group proposes to do by way of achieving them, and we ought not to assume that every traditional group opposes their achievement.

In conclusion, let's consider once more James's comments on a new polytheism. James (1902/1958) speculated briefly (at the end of *Varieties of Religious Experience*) on a universe populated by better, godlike selves "of which the present self would then be but the mutilated expression" (p. 396). Such a notion of God is very like the one advanced by John Dewey (1934).

> "God" means the ideal ends that at a given time and place one acknowledges as having authority over his volition and emotion, the values to which one is supremely devoted, as far as these ends, through imagination, take on unity. (p. 42)

Is this notion of God attractive, or is it so far from traditional definition and so divorced from the longing that calls forth God that we should reject it? Sidney Hook (1961) puts the question:

> Is, then, the religion of Humanism justified in using the term "God" for its conception of the moral enterprise? John Dewey answered the question affirmatively. I answer it negatively. Each one of my readers must answer it for himself. (p. 141)

That, of course, is exactly where we as teachers must leave our students.

CHAPTER 3

Belonging

It is not only interest in existential and metaphysical questions that causes people to choose or reject religion. Affiliation with a religious institution or group is influenced not only by belief in supreme beings but also by a set of related beliefs. Some people believe, for example, that religion is an essential force for good in the world; hence they become members of religious institutions. Others believe that religion is an evil and that humankind must learn to live without it. Still others believe in a supreme being (or beings) but find organized religion too weak or deficient to satisfy their spiritual needs. Most people long to be part of a group they believe is worthy; from this group, they seek approval and affiliation. Intelligent believers have to decide whether or not to join or to remain affiliated with formal religious groups, and sometimes intelligent unbelievers join religious groups even though they do not share their doctrinal beliefs. Most of the material discussed in this chapter might be part of a social studies program.

TO BELONG OR NOT TO BELONG

Belonging to a religion is not always the conscious result of thinking through and coming to believe in what the religion teaches. As Jerome Nathanson (1963) has pointed out:

Many people join a church out of habit, or out of respect for their parents, or for family tradition. Some do so in order to wear the badge of respectability, or get a testimonial to good character. Businessmen and professional men often prize the "contacts" they make in church or a temple; their careers are helped if they conform to the community's values. Some parents want their children to "belong," to do what others in the group do, to associate with the "right" people, to make a good marriage with a decent and moral spouse. (p. 213)

Such reasons for joining a church are not necessarily unintelligent. In fact, they often demonstrate a form of practical or instrumental intelligence, but they do not suggest the sort of reflective intelligence that we hope to encourage in our attempts to educate. It does seem that, to be whole human beings, we must affiliate ourselves with the communities in which we are located. As Paul Tillich (1952) says, it is through participation in these communities that the world is mediated.

> Therefore he who has the courage to be as a part has the courage to affirm himself as a part of the community in which he participates. His self-affirmation is a part of the self-affirmation of the social groups which constitute the society to which he belongs. (p. 91)

The need to belong can be satisfied, of course, by membership in nonreligious groups. In many times and places, however, religious affiliation has been important in achieving general acceptance. Just a few years ago, former president Richard Nixon observed that it would probably be impossible for a confessed unbeliever to win election to the American presidency. Believing is, thus, a test one must pass for political acceptability, and the easiest way to demonstrate belief—without engaging in either dialogue or reflection—is to join a church or synagogue.

Religion is important, then, on both the individual and social levels. On the individual level, religion represents the connection between humans and divinity; it is the realm in which the deepest metaphysical and existential questions are engaged. The Japanese philosopher Nishida (1990) remarks:

> People often ask why religion is necessary. This is identical to asking why we need to live. Religion does not exist apart from the life of the self, and the religious demand is the demand of life itself. Our questions about the necessity of religion reflect a lack of seriousness in our own life. Those who try to think seriously cannot help but feel an intense religious demand. (p. 152)

But the quest for affiliation is at least as strong as the quest for meaning. A. N. Wilson (1991), in his brief "counter blast" at religion, notes:

The believer is in pursuit of something much more palatable and attractive than truth: it is the feeling of being loved—"Ransomed, healed, restored, forgiven, Who like me His praise shall sing?" (p. 28)

People may be born into a religious tradition and simply remain with it because it satisfies either a religious or a social need, or—as suggested in the Wilson quote—both. The need to be loved or at least accepted by other human beings can be satisfied, and the need for a transcendent love can also be met. Both of these needs can be examined reflectively, and for most young people, school is the only setting in which such reflection can be accomplished with sufficient depth and sensitivity. One product of this reflection should be self-knowledge that might prevent many of the horrors historically associated with blind allegiance.

Why do people attach themselves to religious and various political movements? If the answer is "existential longing," then we might expect seekers to cast about for the right gods and the best movements, and we would also expect serious attempts at constructing criteria for making the relevant judgments. Students should be encouraged to explore other possibilities. Here is a quotation from Eric Hoffer (1951) that might start a lively discussion.

The less justified a man is in claiming excellence for his own self, the more ready he is to claim all excellence for his nation, his religion, his race or his holy cause. (p. 23)

Hoffer is talking here about "the true believer," a person who exhibits fanatical devotion to a cause, and surely all of us can point to people who fit his description. Followers in many organizations seem to be of just this type—people who can find self-affirmation only in a group to which they attach themselves completely. But what about leaders? Students might be encouraged to study the biographies of leaders in their own (or other) religions or in great political movements. Do leaders, too, show signs of low self-esteem? Erik Erikson's biographies of Luther and Gandhi come to mind here, but there are many, many others that would be suitable, including the devastating description of Gandhi by Grenier mentioned in Chapter 2.

Hoffer (1951) also flings out a challenge to those who might claim altruistic motives for their religious engagement.

The burning conviction that we have a holy duty toward others is often a way of attaching our drowning selves to a passing raft. What looks like giving a hand is often a holding on for dear life. Take away our holy duties and you leave our lives puny and meaningless. There is no doubt that in exchanging a self-centered for a selfless life we gain enormously in self-esteem. The vanity of the selfless, even those who practice utmost humility, is boundless. (p. 23)

Students may be able to meet Hoffer's challenge by pointing to givers who know and accept the fact that they, too, profit by giving a helping hand. The long and beautiful tradition that teaches that one must lose oneself in order to find oneself might be defended. Indeed, many of us would argue today that the analytical distinction between altruism and egoism is a false dichotomy based on faulty ontology (Noddings, 1984, 1989). And yet there is something in what Hoffer says. Critical readers may point out that he was careful to say that a "burning conviction" of our "holy duties" is *often* a way of saving ourselves. This leaves the door open for alternatives. Again, self-knowledge may help us to accept ways of being that contribute to both ourselves and others.

It is not only self-knowledge that is gained in reflecting on religious participation. Social and political knowledge can also be acquired. Different segments of society look at religion differently and find different uses for it. Evidentially held belief often plays but a minor role. A. R. Rodger (1982) quotes a wise old Irish priest who said of his parishioners:

> "They believe three things, simultaneously. They believe what the Church teaches, about the immortality of the soul, the resurrection of the body, reward and punishment. They also believe that when you are dead you are dead, like an animal, and that's that. And finally they believe that the dead are there, under the ground, watching the living, and plotting malevolently about them." (p. 7)

The priest's comment about contemporary Irish Catholics is reminiscent of one made by Edward Gibbon in *The Decline and Fall of the Roman Empire.*

> "The various modes of worship which prevailed in the Roman world were all considered by the people as equally true; by the philosophers as equally false; and by the magistrates as equally useful." (quoted in Haught, 1990, p. 219)

These observations suggest that unreflective belief is often used by leaders for political purposes. Opinion is divided on whether its uses are mainly good or bad, but most observers agree that the influence of religion in political life is considerable. Indeed, in his multi-volume history of the United States, Page Smith (1984) says:

> It is a major premise of this work that religion is not simply a topic among topics but the driving force of American history, that without close attention to Protestant Christianity it is impossible to make sense of our past. (p. 554)

Many contemporary critics agree with Smith and complain that today's social studies texts give students a skewed picture of history by almost ignoring religion. It seems to me that the critics are right on this, but I would go even further. Not only do students leave school with a faulty impression of history but they miss entirely the special opportunities for reflection that we have been discussing. Religion connects individual, personal life to social life in a unique and powerful way. Wilson (1991) comments:

> Religion appeals to something deep and irrational and strong within us, and this is what makes it so dangerous. If it were not so good, it would not be capable of being so bad. If it did not promise to unite us to God himself, it would not allow us the arrogance and self-righteousness which are its almost inevitable concomitants. (p. 3)

Students need to hear about the ambiguous effects and—Wilson would say—the ambiguous nature of religion. Smith (1984), for example, discusses the leadership of Christians in abolishing slavery. Examining the same era, James Haught (1990) notes with disgust that almost half of the published defenses of slavery were written by ministers. Rubbing salt in the wound, Haught tells us that the well-known slaver, Sir John Hawkins, named his slave ships *Jesus*, *Angel*, and *Grace of God* (p. 223). Is the weight of evidence for or against religion in the matter of slavery and abolition? Surely students should hear both sides of the story and engage in some genuine investigation.

Before turning to a brief discussion of religion as good and then religion as evil, we should acknowledge that, just as there are many reasons for joining religious institutions, there are many for *not* joining. Some people are just too lazy or too indifferent or too occupied with other matters. For some, the need for affiliation is satisfied in other ways. Some disengage themselves from religion because they no longer believe in what it teaches. Some, like Wilson, come to believe that religion is essentially, inherently evil. And others—many others, confess a deep spiritual longing that formal religion fails to satisfy. Nathanson (1963) writes:

> Most of the millions who do not go to church *are* religious. Many have a profound faith in God; they simply do not believe that any existing organized religion is a satisfactory expression of God's will. (p. 215)

How do these people satisfy their spiritual longing? How do they guide their ethical lives? What is it they distrust in organized religion? These questions will be addressed in later chapters. In the rest of this chapter, I will lay out some of the evidence for religion as good and religion as evil.

RELIGION AS A SOCIAL GOOD

No one would deny that religion often inspires people to do generous and wonderful things. Students should certainly read about Mother Teresa, Albert Schweitzer, and the priests and nuns who work tirelessly today in Central America. As they hear these stories, they can be encouraged to find Lambarene, Calcutta, Nicaragua, and El Salvador on maps. Biographical studies can be extended to a study of early and medieval martyrs and to religious heroes of the nineteenth and twentieth centuries.

Having acknowledged that religion sometimes inspires people to help others even at tremendous cost to themselves, we still face the question whether religion itself is a social good or a social evil. Is there something inherently good about religion? Is there something inherently bad? Careful thinkers have answered both questions affirmatively.

One argument for the goodness of religion centers on ethical life. Many argue that religion is necessary for moral life—that without it, people would indulge every base and cruel passion. When this possibility was posed for Bertrand Russell (1963), he responded:

> The existence of base and cruel passions is undeniable, but I find no evidence in history that religion has opposed these passions. On the contrary, it has sanctified them, and enabled people to indulge them without remorse. . . . What appears to justify persecution is dogmatic belief. . . . The spirit of tolerance which some modern Christians regard as essentially Christian is, in fact, a product of the temper which allows doubt and is suspicious of absolute certainties. I think that anybody

who surveys past history in an impartial manner will be driven to the conclusion that religion has caused more suffering than it has prevented. (p. 201)

It seems to me that Russell is basically right on this, and we will discuss some of religion's greatest horrors in the next section. But he is not entirely right. Religion is not necessary for ethical life—as Russell and countless others have demonstrated in their own good lives. But religion has often disseminated a message of love, inspiring many to work passionately for brotherhood. Contemporary Christians, acknowledging a gift of grace, risk their lives for peace and brotherhood in Central America (McNeill, Morrison, & Nouwen, 1983). Members of the Social Gospel movement in the nineteenth century identified sin with conflict between individuals and the good of humanity. They even rejected the divinity of Jesus and concentrated on the example of his human goodness interpreted as a call to all people of good will to battle injustice, greed, and isolation (Cave, 1946). Sufis insist that sin against man is worse than sin against God. Confucians also judge people by their works and not their professed beliefs.

Earlier I mentioned the ambiguous role of Christianity in slavery and abolition. Although Haught (1990) is right when he claims that ministers often advanced biblical defenses for slavery, the historical record also shows Christians in the forefront of the abolition movement. Page Smith (1984) writes, "The battle fought by abolitionists against slavery was fought unequivocally in the name of Christian brotherhood" (p. 554). As I suggested before, this is an excellent topic for students to study in some depth.

Smith (1984) raises a point with respect to abolition that is too often overlooked, and it is a point that has significance well beyond the particular problems of abolition. He draws our attention to the effects of social movements on families and the attitudes of later generations.

> While historians have recently given more weight to the role of individuals in the fight against slavery, they have paid far less attention to the effect of that agitation on the agitators. It now seems clear that the rigors of the struggle, the obloquy and public hostility that the abolitionists and their families endured, the verbal and physical violence constantly directed against them produced a quality of mind and character that proved singularly enduring and that distinguished the members of such families generation after generation by a reformist zeal and the will capable of sustaining it. (p. 914)

Here is another marvelous historical project for students. Who were the prominent abolitionists and how did their families distinguish themselves? In a similar vein, students might trace the family histories of nineteenth century missionaries. The stories are fascinating and the accomplishments quite extraordinary (see Grimshaw, 1983). Although the effects of missionary work in Hawaii, China, and Africa were sometimes horrible, they were sometimes beautiful, and the effects on children raised in missionary households were often remarkable. Many of our own country's political leaders grew up in such households.

Students can profit from discussion of the ambiguous effects of Christianity throughout U.S. history. Robert Bellah and his colleagues (1985) have explored the debilitating effects of individualism on both public and private life. They point approvingly to an early communitarian spirit. Here they quote John Winthrop, Puritan governor of the Massachusetts Bay Colony, from his well-known "A Model of Christian Charity."

> "We must delight in each other, make others conditions our own, rejoyce together, mourn together, labor and suffer together, always having before our eyes our community as members of the same body." (quoted in Bellah et al., 1985, p. 28)

It is this spirit that the writers of *Habits of the Heart* would like to recapture. They go on to warn:

> But if we owe the meaning of our lives to biblical and republican traditions of which we seldom consciously think, is there not the danger that the erosion of these traditions may eventually deprive us of that meaning altogether? (Bellah et al., 1985, p. 82)

Like many others, Bellah and his colleagues identify religion with moral standards and a moral community. In contrast, Haught (1990) looks at the Puritan era and sees something far less admirable.

> They created a religious police state where doctrinal deviation could lead to flogging, pillorying, banishment, hanging—or cutting off ears, or boring through the tongue with a hot iron. Preaching Quaker beliefs was a capital offense. Four stubborn Quakers defied this law and were hanged. In the 1690s, fear of witches seized the colony. Twenty alleged witches were killed and 150 imprisoned. (pp. 123–124)

Haught, because he is documenting "holy horrors," overlooks the beauty of Winthrop's vision. Bellah, because he is arguing for a return to biblical and republican traditions, overlooks the exclusivity and cruelty that pervade both.

The majority of people today regard religion as a force for good in both personal and community life (Stark & Bainbridge, 1985). It is impossible to ignore the multitude of stories affirming the positive effects of religion on personal lives, and many still insist that the main effects are admirable for community and public life as well. Christians point to the lovely words of St. Paul: Noting first that "the flesh" is subject to all sorts of dreadful acts and attitudes—"envyings, murders, drunkenness, revellings, and such like"—he then says, "But the fruit of the Spirit is love, joy, peace, longsuffering, gentleness, goodness, faith, Meekness, temperance" (Galatians 5:22-23). Surely this is a message heard repeatedly in Christian churches.

Critics advise, however, that readers examine the verses immediately preceding those just quoted. In these (Galatians 5:19-20), Paul condemns the sexual misdeeds associated with flesh and also "idolatry, witchcraft, hatred, variance, emulations, wrath, strife, seditions, heresies." He adds that "they which do such things shall not inherit the kingdom of God." It is this perpetual separating of the sheep from the goats that worries critics like Wilson. If Christians are admonished not to hate, they are also called to destroy wickedness—and, often, the wicked themselves. Wilson urges us to consider whether the faults we see in religion are errors—results of human misunderstanding of religious teachings—or defects inherent in the very notion of religion.

James Fowler (1991) reminds us again of the positive effects of religious community.

> Where else in our age-stage segregated era do you have communities where three or four generations interact across age and stage barriers . . . ? What other communities are constituted as *ecologies of care* and *ecologies of vocation*, where people call forth and confirm each other's gifts and giftedness for the service of God . . . ? Where else will you encounter the generativity and generosity that characterize congregational life at its best . . . ? In what other community do people work at seeing each other whole, offsetting the societal reduction of the person to customer, client, patient, student, boss or employee, or sucker in the marketplace? (p. 149)

My own response to Fowler's impressive set of questions is that the school also could and should be such a community, but it need not displace the church. We have to reject the worst elements of functionalism and accept the possibility that some functions must be served by many institutions and that most institutions have multiple purposes and functions. But Fowler recalls to mind, as do Bellah and his colleagues (1985), the positive traditions of religion. If religion is lost, how will community as described here survive? Fowler (1991) goes on to ask:

> What other community works at forming deep emotions of goodness in persons—emotions of the love of God and love of neighbor—and tries to shape the virtues requisite for discipleship? In what other community do persons offer outpourings of presence and support, at least in tangible symbols of food and assistance, when there is death, tragedy, severe illness, or relational rupture? (p. 149)

Besides the traditionally recognized general (and positive) effects of religion on personal and community life, there are special stories to be told. The story of the black church in America is one that all students should hear. Black people, having Christianity foisted on them as slaves, might well have rejected the message along with the messengers. Instead they built an impressive and distinctive form of Christianity that has provided support and bolstered esteem.

Recognizing this remarkable achievement should not blind us to the fact that many African Americans reject Christianity, as Tom Skinner (1970) says, "because, in their view, those who practice religious piety are among the leading exponents of hate, bigotry and prejudice" (p. 11). Skinner remarks, "They feel that these 'Bible-toting saints' perpetuate the most segregated hour of the week—the eleven o'clock Sunday morning" (p. 11). Further, as we will see in Chapter 6, many black leaders rejected Christianity because they believed it perpetuated dependence and illusion.

Nevertheless, the black church represents a powerful version of Christianity. Skinner (1970) writes:

> The black church is the most powerful social institution in the black community. It has been the only place that black people could have power and exercise control without white intervention. It was here that we played politics and economics, and all the things that we were not able to do in the wider society. (p. 71)

We also get a sense of political and economic action in the black church through James Baldwin's novels. In *Go Tell It on the Mountain* (1953), we see the tremendous influence of preachers and "mothers" in the black community. Sometimes, as in all other religious institutions, preachers wield too much power and are themselves less than models of moral purity. John, the young hero of *Go Tell It on the Mountain*, has to struggle against such a corrupt force in the person of his preacher-father.

But the influence of the church is often dramatically good. Skinner (1970) describes his own transformation from a tough, murderous gang chief to a Christian minister and leader. As a black leader, he now becomes involved in boycotts, rent strikes, and other legitimate protests. Further, he says:

> I am involved in trying to get the schools in my community decentralized so that black kids will be able to go to school with black leadership and grow up understanding that there are leaders who are black, so that they can learn something about themselves, so that the people in the black community will have some control over their political and social and economic destiny, because that is a matter of justice. (p. 78)

For Skinner, Christianity is absolutely essential in furnishing the foundation for community. He says that the gospel of Jesus solves the problem of community.

> I now know who my neighbor is: He is any person I come into contact with, he is all the people of the world. And my attitude toward my neighbor has definitely changed because I know who I am. A man who knows who he is can certainly get along with people. (p. 82)

Baldwin's John also goes through a conversion experience, but his is a terrifying, convulsive spell on the "threshing-floor" before the altar. Here John suffers the soul-separation of hell, the utter helplessness of the human condition and, finally, a sense of salvation, communion, and commitment. He is surrounded by a supportive community to which he will contribute significantly.

Discussion of the black church provides a context for deeper exploration of black history and its connection to "American" history. Christianity too often supported slavery—first by making it all right to enslave non-Christians, later (when many blacks had been baptized) by finding biblical verses that would permit the practice on the basis of color. Even when religion and its effects are discussed in social studies classes, the influence of the black church on mainstream white religion is often overlooked. W. E. B. DuBois (1978) comments:

Moreover, the religious growth of millions of men, even though they be slaves, cannot be without potent influence upon their contemporaries. The Methodists and Baptists of America owe much of their condition to the silent but potent influence of their millions of Negro converts. Especially is this noticeable in the South, where theology and religious philosophy are on this account a full half century behind the North, and where the religion of the poor whites is a plain copy of Negro thought and methods. The mass of "Gospel" hymns which has swept through American churches and well-nigh ruined our sense of song, consists largely of debased imitations of Negro melodies made by ears that caught the jingle but not the music, the body but not the soul, of the Jubilee songs. (p. 216)

Sometimes people recommend greater attention to religion in schools because they believe the United States was established as a Christian nation. In an era when the intentions of the nation's founders are so often invoked, it would be valuable for students to learn a bit about the founding fathers and why it is so difficult to determine their intentions. Russell Kirk (1989), for example, says that it is easy to determine the intent of the founders with respect to religion. He insists that all but three or four were Christians and that order, justice, and freedom are religious concepts. This was to be a religious nation, he declares, and democracy cannot thrive without this recognition. In direct contradiction, Barbara Ehrenreich (1989) says that religious values tend to undermine democracy. She says that the founding fathers did not intend to establish a "Christian nation" because "they were, for the most part, not Christians at all" (p. 82). She then points to evidence that Jefferson, Franklin, Madison, and probably even Washington were deists—not Christians—and that Washington "approved the 1797 Treaty with Tripoli that stated unequivocally, 'The government of the United States is not in any sense founded on the Christian religion'" (p. 82). Students should be encouraged to explore the beliefs of the founders on both religion and slavery.

Those who insist that democracy is necessarily rooted in religion (in Christianity) are no doubt afraid that, if religion is allowed to fade away, certain cherished values will also disappear, and this is an issue students should consider in some depth. But the contemporary religious revival may have little to do with democracy, brotherhood, charity, or any moral values at all. Ehrenreich (1989) puts it this way:

The reason why so many Americans have been "born again" is probably not too different from the reason why young Arabs have been taking to Islamic fundamentalism, or why some American Jews are returning to orthodox Judaism. As the recently religious say, religion provides rules, a ready-made community, and a sense of belonging to something more lasting than a swirl of consumer culture. (p. 80)

As we noted at the beginning of this section, these are not necessarily poor or unintelligent reasons for joining a religious institution, but the closing statement in Ehrenreich's paragraph gives us cause to demand deeper reasons.

Religion can also endow the rest of one's beliefs and opinions with an inarguable kind of sanctity, and this is as true on the growing religious left as on the religious right. (p. 80)

This tendency to sanctify a set of beliefs in light of central absolutes is convincingly documented by Alan Peshkin. Believing in their own interpretation of Christianity as *God's* view, the fundamentalists Peshkin studied regretfully pronounced him doomed unless he were to accept Christ and be born again. Peshkin (1986) comments:

Fundamentalist Christians make me aware of my existence and my potential nonexistence, or disappearance. When anyone believes that Jews are doomed, imperfect, incomplete, their prayers not heard by God, I hear whispers of disappearance in these arrogant perceptions. (p. 287)

Peshkin notes that such arrogant attitudes are especially dangerous when they are joined to secular power, and this is a warning all students should hear.

RELIGION AS EVIL

A. N. Wilson (1991) starts his brief treatise *Against Religion* by saying:

It is said in the Bible that the love of money is the root of all evil. It might be truer to say that the love of God is the root of all evil. Religion is the tragedy of mankind. (p. 1)

Noting that all religions claim they worship a God of Peace, believe in love for humankind, and so on, he adds:

Although this argument is about as convincing as the plea that Rottweilers make friendly family pets if they are only treated in the right

way . . . religious people can nearly always be sure of a tolerant hearing
when they say it. We are so frightened of offending the religious sensi-
bilities of other people that we do not like to ask them the awkward
question. Why does so much unhappiness and bloodshed and conflict
occur in the name of religion if it is so essentially good and peaceable a
thing? . . . Surely, it needs to be said that all this evil does not stem
from a perversion of religion but from religion itself, from pure religion
and undefiled? It stems from the religious person's belief in God and
his belief in absolutes. (p. 10)

Now even if we find religion, on balance, more good than evil,
and even if we would prefer to sort through religions rather than
condemn them wholesale, Wilson's point about God and absolutes
is an important one to explore. He recounts with chagrin the attitude
of well-educated Christians like J. R. R. Tolkien, who insisted that
"God's law" applies to all—believers and nonbelievers, Christians,
Jews, Muslims, and atheists. If there were such a thing as "God's
law," Tolkien would of course be right. The difficulty is that people
disagree on whether such law exists. Further, and more important
in practical affairs, they disagree on the content of such law. Some
extremely difficult social controversies resist resolution on just this
account. For example, if one believes that God's law forbids abortion,
then clearly it forbids abortion for everyone. Such a believer cannot
accept choice as an option. There is no possibility that abortion can
be wrong for her but right for me. The insistence on absolutes and
the added claim to privileged knowledge about these absolutes con-
tradict the great Enlightenment pronouncements on intellectual and
moral freedom. Hence Wilson (1991) concludes, in opposition to writers who find religion a positive force, that the heralded comeback of
religion is "bad news for the human race" (p. 20).

It is not just a handful of contemporary philosophers and novel-
ists who find religion evil. In the eighteenth century, Voltaire worked
hard to save prisoners condemned by religious courts. In one case,
the best he could do was to save a teenager, whose crime was mere
disrespect for a religious procession, from horrible torture and slow
death. The boy was, nevertheless, decapitated. Voltaire said straight
out:

"Every sensible man, every honorable man, must hold the Christian
sect in horror. [It] is the most ridiculous, the most absurd, and bloody
religion that has ever infected the world." (quoted in Haught, 1990,
p. 131)

Haught's book, *Holy Horrors*, is filled cover to cover with stories and pictures of religious killings—killings of heretics, Jews, Anabaptists, Catholics (by Protestants), Protestants (by Catholics), witches, and others unfortunate enough to cross the religious hierarchy. Nor does he spare religions other than Christianity; Aztec sacrifices were regular bloodbaths, and Hindu-Muslim massacres have been numerous. During the Crusades—thought to be holy wars by both sides—Christians catapulted the heads of Muslim soldiers into enemy cities, and Muslims fired Christian heads back. Haught's account is a sickening parade of torture, hanging, burning, drowning, cutting, and mutilation of human beings by other human beings convinced that they were doing God's will.

The harm done by people in the name of religion can be described at several levels. First, there is the historical record, made vivid by Haught, of holy horrors—of group against group or group against individual. One might think that this level of harm is the easiest to change and that "progress" gradually eliminates it. As we have seen, this is doubtful. Second, there is the kind of harm described by Alice Miller (1983) done to individuals whose religious upbringing produces warped and unhappy people. Often the people who experience such upbringing cannot remember—without the help of analysis—the most awful things that happened to them and, when they can, they usually affirm their own mistreatment; that is, they believe the cruelties visited on them were really for their own good. Third, religion collaborates in the general practices of child rearing and, thus, has effects not only on individuals but on whole communities and societies. Both Haught (1990) and Miller (1983) trace much of the Nazi horror to rigid forms of Christian upbringing. Fourth, religion and the attitude of deference we are taught to have for it create intellectual blindspots. Even people who are demonstrably capable of skeptical analysis in various academic disciplines are often unable to challenge religious dogma and, when they are able to do so, they are still incapable of analyzing religion's indirect effects and inherent faults. We are all taught to avoid Wilson's awkward question.

The first harm, intergroup violence, is at least in part a product of how people construe their gods and is, thus, related to the discussion in Chapter 2. Psychologically, it is healthier to attribute both good and evil to God, as Jews often do, than to insist on the all-goodness of God. In all holy books, there are passages that speak directly of godly wrath, vengeance, and favoritism. When these passages are repressed—as they often are in Christian churches—violent, religiously inspired feelings may lie dormant. But violence is part of the history of all major religions, and the desire to destroy the wicked can be easily aroused. For some groups, the wicked must have performed horrible acts in order to qualify as "wicked," thereby deserving retribution. For others, the wicked are simply those who do not believe or believe differently. In the latter case, violence may be direct and physical if religious belief is combined with political power, or, in the absence of such power, it may be threatened at some later date—for example, at the second coming. In this case, those threatening destruction can be relieved of their own violent feelings and even gain a measure of self-righteousness by warning unbelievers of the impending disaster (Bloom, 1992).

Present attempts to revise Christianity along lines that emphasize love, brotherhood, and solidarity may or may not succeed. Many Christian thinkers protest that such a movement is not a revision but a return to Christian origins. Here we must distinguish between the teachings of Jesus and the various practices of Christianity. But even the teachings of Jesus require interpretation and invite the kind of well-intentioned cruelty often found in missionary zeal. Certainly both revision and return should be studied, but the possibility of their success cannot be evaluated without a study of theodicy. As we saw in Chapter 2, strict monotheists cannot explain the presence of evil in the world without attributing it to either God or human beings. Schemes such as the Augustinian one put the onus on human beings and, thus, give us a reason for acting against each other. Revisioning God as a fallible God is, psychologically, a step in the right direction, but it has never been attractive to Christians. Another possibility, to be explored more fully in Chapter 6, is to encourage religious humanism.

R. C. Zaehner (1974) notes that the "Christ-event" was supposed to move human beings from a violent to a loving vision of God. But the event seems not to have accomplished that purpose.

> Man is just as wicked, mediocre, and stupid as he ever was. And the reason is, I suspect, that we are all Marcionites (or Buddhists, there is not much difference) at heart. We do not believe in the reality of the raving God, despite the fact that those few of us who have any intelligence at all realize that he is raving within ourselves all the time. (p. 233)

This is a complex statement. It is related to Jung's call for an integrated god—one incorporating both good and evil. But, whereas Jung saw the need for further integration—the inclusion of the feminine in the deity in order to manage divine omniscience—Zaehner simply urges acceptance of the savage God and understanding of the "Christ-event" as a demonstration that evil can be overcome or redirected by good. He ignores the fact that the evil he sees and accepts in God will be construed as good by most people. They will strongly resist the idea of a fallible God and will continue to use the distorted God-image as a model for their own behavior. Resistance to the idea of a fallible God is tied up with the second harm associated with religion.

Just as people resist the idea of a fallible God or gods, many people refuse to acknowledge the shortcomings of their own parents. Such refusal is a mark of serious illness and is well documented in psychoanalysis. Alice Miller (1983) makes the connection explicitly.

> Can it ever occur to a small child that the need for thunder and lightning [parental rage] arises from the unconscious depths of the adult psyche and has nothing to do with his or her own psyche? The biblical quotation, "For whom the Lord loveth, he correcteth," implies that the adult shares in the divine omnipotence, and just as the truly devout person is not to question God's motives (see the Book of Genesis), so too the child is supposed to defer to the adult without asking for explanations. (p. 39)

Both Miller and Hoffer (1951) are wary of those who claim immoderate excellence for their gods, parents, political groups, or causes.

The danger in all these cases—besides the unhappiness and misery of neurosis—is that the devoted adherent often internalizes the oppressor. The cruelties suffered or demanded become justified, and the sufferer tends to avenge his treatment by repeating it. Projecting his own weakness and supposed faults onto vulnerable others, he continues his own punishment by inflicting it on others. The cases Miller presents are embedded in Christian traditions, but Christianity is not the only religion that can be so indicted.

Zaehner (1974) analyzes the case of Charles Manson and Eastern religion. Manson, says Zaehner, misunderstood Eastern religion when he adopted the notion that "everything is the same" or "all is one." For Manson this meant that "killing is the same as being killed" and that, ultimately, nothing that happens to human bodies matters. Manson might indeed have found the savage God in Eastern religions—Hindu, Muslim, or Sikh thought—God as a Thug and advisor to the cult of Kali, a group that murdered without pity or remorse. In addition, many passages in Hindu thought suggest that fear of killing and being killed should be laid aside. For example, Krishna advises the warrior Arjuna to enter a fierce battle even though he has relatives on the opposing side. Krishna's argument is that every life extends backward and forward into eternity. What ill-schooled cultists like Manson overlook is that the warrior is to fight in a good cause. And, of course, he totally misses the blend of spirituality, daily life, and political activism that we find in Gandhi's teaching.

> Gandhi's experiments in truth offer a life of practical struggle informed by spiritual aspirations that see everyday experiences as challenges to the will and imagination. Domestic problems cease to be distractions from the great work and become object lessons in the power of ahimsa. Simple creeds and religious formulas renew themselves when applied directly to new political controversies. (Inchausti, 1991, pp. 27–28)

But one might argue that Manson was ruined not by either his knowledge or ignorance of *Eastern* religion. What little he knew merely provided aphorisms and slogans. If religion had any hand in his ruin, it was exactly the religion Zaehner (1974) so paradoxically defends. Here it is in frightening form.

> Of course God knows he is asking us to do what he alone can do, "to kill the thing he loves," which our savage God is doing throughout eternity, because in him, *and in him alone*, Heraclitus' paradox is true: "Justice *is* strife," and life *is* death, and self-sacrifice *is* self-fulfillment. This certainly is sheer "stupidity" and "silliness" to the intellectuals, but Christ made it very plain that he was not interested in them but in silly little children (nepios) who would do what they were told, or at least try to. What he is telling us from the cross is this: . . . My father has killed me because I am his second self. He has killed me and, in killing me, he has killed himself. But he cannot die because he is pure, unchanging "form." I can: because the matter that made it possible for me to become a social animal . . . I took from my mother Mary who willingly accepted the common lot of our chosen Jewish race which is to kiss the hand that strikes us. She knew and did not flinch when old Simeon prophesied that "a sword will pierce your own soul too." She accepted everything on your behalf because she was the kind of silly little child I love. You can do the same, but only with my help. (pp. 299–300)

Many critics of Christianity find passages of this sort horrifying. The acceptance—even glorification—of sacrifice, the unreasoned submission, the masochism, the elevation of childlike faith—all present great difficulties for both intelligent believers and intelligent unbelievers. Charles Manson grew up in a society rife with hypocrisy—one in which children suffer cruel deprivation while, at the same time, they are bombarded with messages of goodness and love. Manson was quite willing to kill what he once might have loved in himself, quite ready to equate life with death. He was not, however, ready to kiss the hand that had struck him repeatedly. From the perspective provided by Alice Miller (1983), Manson had entirely lost the capacity to gain access to his true self. Authorities in his life were very like the savage God—perpetrating cruelty after cruelty and expecting gratitude in return. Whether his own terrible crimes should be partially excused because of their possible origins is a topic we will discuss in Chapter 7.

The positive effects of religion on individuals are often direct and available to us through personal testimony. Tom Skinner and Baldwin's John are examples. The negative effects are usually indirect, and religion can rarely be singled out as the only cause of cruelty and neurosis. However, religion collaborates in child rearing and education and, through this collaboration, has effects on whole generations and societies. Miller (1983), concentrating on "poisonous pedagogies," includes the contributions of Protestant Christianity to the poison potion.

Miller (1983) claims that susceptibility to Fascism is traceable to forms of strict upbringing typically endorsed by German Protestantism. She writes, "Among all the leading figures of the Third Reich, I have not been able to find a single one who did not have a strict and rigid upbringing" (p. 65). That religion was involved in this rigidity is clear in the statements of many of the Nazi high command. It is also frighteningly clear in a statistic offered by Miller: "60% of German terrorists in recent years have been the children of Protestant ministers" (p. 65). Here is a problem for educators to study in some depth: In what circumstances do the families of highly religious parents turn to admirable forms of social action (as many abolitionists' children did) and when do they turn to methods totally unacceptable to the stated doctrines of the traditions within which they have been raised? What role can education play in ameliorating the worse and encouraging the better effects of a religious upbringing?

The problem just mentioned is particularly appropriate for educators because, it seems, the usual forms of education leave the ill effects of religion untouched or actually exacerbate them. Miller (1983) writes:

> Both Hitler and Stalin had a surprisingly large number of enthusiastic followers among intellectuals. Our capacity to resist has nothing to do

with our intelligence but with the degree of access to our true self. Indeed, intelligence is capable of innumerable rationalizations when it comes to the matter of adaptation. Educators have always known this and have exploited it for their own purposes. (p. 43)

I do not mean to suggest that Miller's thesis is airtight or perfect. She puts perhaps too exclusive an emphasis on child rearing, neglecting other influences on the development of social attitudes, and she does not explore fully enough the mechanisms by which some people retain their humanity despite rigid upbringing. But her evidence is impressive, and her challenge to education should be heeded. It is startling and frightening that so many religiously reared, highly educated persons could participate in such horrendous acts.

Haught, too, sees a religious (Christian) influence in the Nazi persecution of Jews. Without the centuries of Christian denigration of Jews, the Nazis might have had a much harder time pressing their case. Religion had prepared the ground for the seeds of hatred and fertilized it with forms of child rearing that prevented even the best educated from questioning authority. Worse, these methods separated people from their own feelings and, thus, from compassion. As Miller points out, many of Germany's intellectuals, quite capable of skeptical questioning in their own fields of study, never dreamed of questioning religious, state, or parental authority. They had been systematically denied access to their true selves and managed to keep what they viewed as morality and decency carefully compartmentalized alongside rationalizations for stomach-turning horrors. People who ran the concentration camps really did sing Christmas carols with their families, defend the rights of animals (Himmler is an example), and turn sentimental while listening to Beethoven and Bach.

Miller says that the Nazis did not experience a loss of autonomy. Rather, autonomy never developed. People raised by such methods will adapt to any form of authority that claims to be legitimate and has the power to make the claim stick. This is what Hoffer (1951), too, says of the true believer. The opposite of right-wing extremism, says Hoffer, is not left-wing extremism but a well-balanced moderation. The fanatic personality may well switch causes, but the fanatic behavior simply finds another outlet.

I will close this section by saying that I would not share all of the psychoanalytic material discussed or implied here with high school students, but I would certainly recommend it for teachers. In today's educational climate, teachers are urged unceasingly to control their students—not only to manage classroom behavior but to prescribe every learning outcome, keep their students on task, evaluate the outcome of every objective, squelch every "random" behavior, and stick rigidly to an authoritatively recommended teaching plan. If teachers understood the company they were in as they adopt (or adapt to?) these methods, they might resist using them. Perhaps we are fortunate that so many students in this country refuse to accept pedagogical authority. There are worse things than cultural illiteracy.

SUMMARY

People belong to religious institutions for a wide variety of reasons. Some of these reasons—such as meeting the right people, finding appropriate companions for one's children, gaining social acceptability—demonstrate practical intelligence, but without reflection on the institution's teachings, we cannot ascribe a healthy level of intelligence. In particular, educators should want people to think carefully about any group they join. Is the group or institution good or bad? On what grounds is the evaluation made? What must I believe to be a legitimate member?

To aid such evaluation, we looked briefly at the effects of religion on individuals, communities, child rearing, and intellectual life. As educators, we cannot demand that students decide whether religion is good, bad, or a mixture of both, but we can hope that the questions we raise will continue to interest them: Does the religious revival in the United States herald a new age of peace, joy, and fulfillment, or is it, as Wilson (1991) insists, "bad news for the human race"?

CHAPTER 4

Feminism and Religion

All high school students should know that there is a political aspect of religion and that, like politics in general, it can serve good or ill purposes. In Chapter 3, we saw that religion has had good and evil effects on both individuals and communities. Here, to give specificity to the connection between religion and politics, we will examine the interaction between feminism and religion.

Students should be at least acquainted with topics in several broad areas: the history and features of patriarchal religion, alternatives in feminist spirituality and goddess religion, and alternatives created through revision of traditional doctrines and rituals. In all of these areas, so much fine contemporary writing exists that teachers need not risk expounding their own views. There is a risk, however, of one-sided presentation. The horrors of patriarchal religion, seen in light of women's awakening, are so great that teachers might fill all the available space with their description and condemnation. Part of our pedagogical task is to dig out, where we can, material that softens the tale of oppression.

PATRIARCHAL RELIGION

All the world's great religions—monotheistic, dualistic, polytheistic—have been, at least in historical times, patriarchal. By "patriarchal" we mean that their doctrines have been developed by males, their offices of power filled by men, their rituals defined and governed by men, their images mainly male, and their female images defined and described by men. We mean also that religions have been part of a larger phenomenon in societies—one in which the male has been the prototype human being and the female an afterthought or alien other.

The patriarchal nature of religion is revealed explicitly in its structures and theologies and implicitly in its literature and poetry. Here is F. W. Bain (1911) introducing his translation of *The Ashes of a God*—explaining why freedom and detachment are so hard for the Hindu sage to achieve.

> And what, then, is it, that is of all things most peculiarly the object of regret; that laughs at all efforts to reduce it to oblivion and nonentity; that refuses to be driven into the *oubliettes* of any soul? Needless to say, a woman. . . . She is regarded, in Oriental mysticism, as beyond all other things the enemy of emancipation; the clog *par excellence*; the fetter of the soul; the everlastingly regretted, the unforgettable and unforgotten, the irreducible residuum; the inextinguishable spark among the ashes of the past. (pp. x–xi)

The construal of woman as other, as enemy of spiritual growth and purity, as enchantress is found in familiar Christian literature as well. Students should hear Tertullian's fiery sermon branding woman as "the Devil's gateway," Jerome's disgust with clean (and, therefore, alluring) bodies (Ruether, 1974), and St. Anthony's terror under his delusional temptations of the flesh (Dijkstra, 1986). We hear in all these accounts a theme to which I will return—that of woman as body and impediment to spirit—but there are other themes that should be part of an adequate education.

The notion that man is the endpoint of evolution is such a theme, one that induces challenging issues on two levels. First, if "man" is defined as humankind, one might challenge the notion on grounds similar to those mentioned earlier in connection with progress. In what sense does the appearance of human beings represent progress? Might humans be just an intermediate species leading eventually to a far more advanced form? Should we think of evolution in terms of progress and advance or simply in terms of chance, adaptation, and random fluctuations that can be labeled advances or setbacks only if we invoke criteria that can be questioned? In an age of tremendous interest in the earth and all its life, these questions are of concern to many groups besides feminists.

On the second level, it is clear that many religious evolutionists in the fin-de-siècle (and even today) really meant "male human being" when they used the term *man*, and it is issues at this level of challenge that especially concern feminists. Women had long suffered discrimination under theological and philosophical theories that claimed the "natural" superiority of male over female. Claims of natural male superiority are found in Aristotle, and Christian theologians used the story of the Fall to add moral superiority to the merely "natural." But in the late nineteenth century, as traditional religion was losing its hold on educated thought, Darwinism gave new strength to Christianity and to the doctrine of male superiority (Dijkstra, 1986). It was held now that evolution had created a great gap between man and woman, and it was predicted that the gap would grow (Spencer, 1873/1909; Vogt, 1874/1969; but see also Hubbard, 1979).

Social Darwinism gave white, Christian males a scientific excuse to exploit (or, euphemistically, "use to the glory of God") those whom evolution had shortchanged. After all, if evolution were God's chosen method for continuous creation, it must be God's will that the "unfit" are as we find them. Evolutionary theism gave support to idealistic nationalism as well. A great Christian nation, marked by its obvious evolutionary success, was meant to lead the backward nations to Christianity, democracy, and capitalism. Significant remnants of that arrogance remain today.

There is an opportunity in this first broad area of concern for students not only to learn about the philosophical and scientific oppression of women but also to reflect on the anthropocentric perspective through which most of us look at the earth. It is at least conceivable that people will some day regard our present attitude as premoral in the same way that we now judge the pre-Copernican attitude as prescientific. It is also conceivable that the place of human beings in the universe is vastly more complex than the movement of heavenly bodies and that nothing we have yet envisioned is morally and practically adequate. I emphasize this possibility because students introduced to the idea that humans may not be the apex of evolution or the ultimate purpose of creation often swing about to adopt theories and practices only half-considered—some of which may actually be injurious to the earth they want to protect.

An offshoot of the belief that humans, and men in particular, are the end of evolution is the notion that those at the top of the hierarchy rightly have the power to name, define, classify, describe, and appropriate everything around them. In Genesis 2, God gives Adam the privilege of naming every living creature, including the woman presented to him as a "help meet."

Until recently, women have argued—when they have been allowed to speak at all—for the right to share in what was perceived as a common language. Today feminists realize that, unless naming is a product of dialogue, it is likely to be at best only partially adequate.

Mary Daly (1974, 1984) has been instrumental in showing us the power of naming and what women have suffered as a result of being deprived of that power. Can it have been as recently as 1973 that she shook the intellectual world with the expression "sisterhood of man"? Daly (1974) wrote:

> "Intellectually" everyone "knows" that "man" is a generic term. However, in view of the fact that we live in a world in which full humanity is attributed only to males, and in view of the significant fact that "man" also means male, the term does not come through as truly generic. . . . What "sisterhood of man" does is to give generic weight to "sisterhood" which the term has never before been called upon to bear. (p. 9)

Other feminists, too, wrote forcefully on the power of language and naming (Spender, 1980), and today academics are pressed by convention to "avoid sexist language." But the struggle goes on to conceive or locate images, name, and describe in the realm of religion and spirituality. More than a decade before Mary Daly's *Beyond God the Father*, Sidney Hook (1961) criticized the "reflective believer" who recognized that neither "person" nor "father" could be applied to God in a literal sense, and yet found "no difficulty in praying to 'Our Father in Heaven.' He would, however, deem it singularly inappropriate for anyone to refer to God in prayer as 'Our Nephew in Heaven.' Why?" (p. 124). Why, indeed? Women have pressed the case for a mother God and some churches echo with prayer that begins, "Dear Father and Mother God," but women are still denied equal participation in many churches, and many women have not found an appropriate image of God by tacking "Mother" onto a name that belongs to an essentially male God.

A third broad concern about patriarchy that should be part of everyone's education is religion's role in maintaining the long association of women with nature, bodies, and contamination. Except for the last—contamination—some of us writing today can write with enthusiasm about women's concern for nature and bodies. But what we write differs greatly from the traditional line. Aristotle described woman as a "misbegotten male" and Aquinas too asked why woman should have been created and found only one reason—to participate in reproduction. Although the sacred texts of Judaism (Bird, 1974), Islam (Hassan, 1990), and Christianity all contain statements that urge respect and fairness for women, heterodox and mythical literatures emphasize the inferiority of women (Hassan, 1990; Phillips,

1984). Further, male believers in all three great religions generally accept the idea that Adam was God's primary creation and that woman was an afterthought—created from Adam, for Adam.

In contrast, Sara Ruddick (1989) gives serious philosophical attention to bodies and notes the absence of such attention in traditional philosophy. Birth, an occasion for celebration in most cultures, is ignored in philosophy. Ruddick writes, "Although we are a species that knows its own natality, in philosophical texts we are 'thrown' into the universe somehow, appearing at the earliest when we can talk and read" (p. 189). In religious texts and rituals, birth is often regarded as a source of pollution and contamination, and the very potential of females for pregnancy is regarded with disgust and ritual wariness (Ruether, 1974).

Christianity has been more guilty than Judaism in demeaning bodies and bodily functions. Judaism resists the glorification of nature that we find in nature religions, but it also rejects the association of the body with sin. Buber comments: "Even when Christianity includes natural life in its sacredness, as in the sacrament of marriage, the bodily life of man is not hallowed but merely made subservient to holiness" (quoted in Friedman, 1991, p. 227). But Judaism, too, has connected women's bodily functions with pollution and contamination.

Another facet of the long association of women with nature and bodily functions that students should be aware of is the attitude of exploitation that has been directed at both. The idea of "wringing nature's secrets" from her, of controlling, dominating, using is echoed in patriarchy's treatment of women. Students interested in forms of nature religion may be delighted to know that some women scientists take an appreciative, listening attitude toward the objects of their study rather than the usual controlling one (Keller, 1983, 1985).

Closely related to the association of women with body and nature, and men with spirit and culture is the notion of women's moral inferiority. As several feminist theologians have pointed out, the claim that women are morally inferior to men was based on women's bodies—not on their education, opportunities, or anything else that could be changed (McLaughlin, 1974; Ruether, 1974). The female body itself demands that all attention go to reproduction; hence, the argument went, first, that women had not the capacity for moral thought and, later, that evolution had perfected the female for sex and motherhood, the male for intellectual and moral creativity. In psychology, Freud argued that women did not develop a superego "so inexorable, so impersonal, so independent of its emotional origins as we require it to be in men" (Sagan, 1988, p. 77) because they did not have to fear castration and, thus, resolve their Oedipus complex by internalizing the voice of the father.

Early theological and mythical accounts actually associated women with evil (Noddings, 1989). From the early Greeks' story of Pandora, who was sent purposely to plague man, to the witch craze of the fifteenth, sixteenth, and seventeenth centuries, we see a mixture of politics and religion in the persecution of women. Certainly thousands, and perhaps millions, of women were accused, tortured, and executed during the witch craze; 80% to 90% of its victims were women, and all died at the hands of a religion that feared and denigrated women. Joseph Klaits (1985) remarks: "The witch craze often has been described as one of the most terrible instances of man's inhumanity to man. But more accurate is the formulation by gender, not genus: witch trials exemplify men's inhumanity to women" (p. 51).

The connections among bodies, women, and evil were made explicit by Sprenger and Kramer in the *Malleus Maleficarum*: "All witchcraft comes from carnal lust, which is in women insatiable" (quoted in Haught, 1990, p. 74). Women's bodies were meticulously searched for a "devil's mark" or "witches' tits." Sex organs were of special interest to the inquisitors, and they were often the focus of torture as well as inspection. (See Haught, 1990.) Is all this mere history? Students should certainly be aware of the history, but they should also know that menstruating females are still considered by several of the world's great religions to be sources of pollution.

Finally, since so much has been derived from it, students should be well acquainted with the story of Adam and Eve and the Fall. Why are current religious myths not included in the school curriculum? Some gods appear, of course, and mythical interpretations of various phenomena are also regularly included in the curriculum. Zeus, Hera, and Hermes are familiar figures in school mythology, and generations of students have been encouraged to learn the Greek/Roman dualities: Zeus/Jupiter, Hera/Juno, Hermes/Mercury. Odin and Loki appear somewhat less frequently, and Anansi, the delightful trickster-spider, even less frequently. But Adam and Eve appear almost never. Giant mythologies, such as Larousse's *World Mythology*, do not even mention Adam or Eve in their index. Yet biblical stories of the Creation and Fall are, by any definition, clearly myths and, given their enormous influence on Western society, one might suppose that they should appear prominently in the literature with which students should have a critical acquaintance. Why do they not?

When I pose this question for students of educational theory, many of them react with shock to the suggestion. These are religious stories that some people still believe, they say. You demean them by calling them "myths." But is this true? Are myths told and believed only by people of long ago or far away? Are there no myths still alive and well in Western culture? Well, respond my startled students, of course—but you can't include *religious* myths in the curriculum; that violates the separation of Church and State.

This response misses the educational point. We should not, of course, teach the Adam and Eve myth to either advance or debunk religion. We should teach it with the purpose of promoting *intelligent* belief or unbelief. If teaching it as a myth is religiously offensive, the feeling of offense is almost certainly caused by a misunderstanding of myth and mythic literature. Here is an opportunity to explain that myths are not untruths or fantasies. Rather, they are stories designed to explain cultural and natural phenomena in such a way that they can be interpreted and reinterpreted over many generations. The power of myths actually grows through a process of demythologization. As Paul Ricoeur (1969) wrote, a myth grows more powerful as it loses its false logos. Therefore, religious myths can be treated with the respect and dignity appropriate to their status in religious life.

To respect the status of myths in religious traditions does not require that they be allowed to escape criticism. Students should hear Ricoeur's (1969) comments on the mischief done by coupling the Adam and Eve myth with Augustine's pronouncements on original sin (p. 239; see Chapter 2, this volume). Again, criticism can be accomplished without having teachers express personal opinions or judgmental statements suggesting that one view is true and another false.

It is important, too, that students be aware of the many stories—both orthodox and heterodox—about the first woman and her role in bringing evil to the world. For example, the early Church Fathers could have ignored the story of Pandora, but they seemed to have encouraged it in the heterodox literature (Phillips, 1984). Even though they labeled it a pagan myth, they used its terms to describe Eve: "vain," "fraudulent," "immodest," "self-seeking," "prurient" (Phillips, 1984, p. 22). They accepted the characterization of both Pandora and Eve as a "beautiful evil."

The creation of Eve is the subject of great art and of folktales.

Phillips (1984) recounts well-known Jewish legends that "may be more humorous or mischievous than vicious, but . . . are nonetheless almost unrelievedly misogynist" (p. 29). Eve was created because the creator foresaw bringing charges against her; when Eve was created, Satan was also created, and Eve's creation was preceded by God's reflection on which part of Adam to use.

> I will not create her from the head, lest she be swellheaded; nor from the eye, lest she be a coquette; nor from the ear, lest she be an eavesdropper; nor from the mouth, lest she be prone to gossip; nor from the hand, lest she be light-fingered; nor from the heart, lest she be prone to jealousy; nor from the foot, lest she be a gadabout; but from the modest part of man, for even when he stands naked, that part is covered. Yet in spite of all this . . . she is swellheaded . . . she is a coquette . . . she is an eavesdropper . . . she is prone to jealousy . . . she is light-fingered . . . she is a gadabout. (quoted in Phillips, 1984, p. 29)

One can argue that the orthodox texts of Judaism, Christianity, and Islam avoid the extremes of misogynist thought, but heterodox literature abounds in it, and this literature clearly affected the selection of orthodox statements that were to be emphasized. The story of Eve's creation from Adam's rib became much more widely accepted and publicized than the first chapter creation story.

Both Jewish and Islamic traditions tell folk stories about Eve's creation. In one, a dog steals Adam's rib before God can create Eve; God then uses the dog's tail to create Eve. In an Islamic tale, Eve is created from the serpent's feet, thus explaining both Eve's turpitude and the serpent's footless condition. Echoing the Pandora story, some heterodox tales even suggest that Eve was expressly created to bring death to Adam (Phillips, 1984, pp. 42–43).

Students should also be exposed to feminist critiques of the myths of Creation and Fall. How do feminists interpret the symbolism of the myths? What do they see as their history? What political purposes were served by their traditional interpretation and promulgation? These questions bring us to the next major topic.

ALTERNATIVES IN FEMINIST SPIRITUALITY

At the very least, students should be aware of feminist analyses of the symbolism in the Adam and Eve myth. What does the creation of Eve from Adam suggest about the centrality of women as creators of life? The theological inclination to regard the processes of conception and birth as tainted with sin appears in both the myth of Adam and the later account of the virgin birth. As Daly (1974) and other feminists have noted, the creation of Eve performs a monumental inversion—producing woman from man instead of man from woman.

The role of the serpent in this myth is especially interesting. Merlin Stone (1976) has documented the place of serpents in earlier woman-centered religions. Many of the statues recovered from this period show goddesses and priestesses entwined with snakes or accompanied by serpents on either side. Sometimes the Goddess herself was even portrayed as a serpent. Apparently, the snake symbolized prophetic wisdom and its appearance in a multitude of artifacts suggests the power of the Serpent Goddess and her priestesses. In addition to its connection to prophetic wisdom, the serpent was also associated with renewal and immortality. Esther Harding (1976) writes, "Primitive and ancient myths . . . relate that the gift of immortality was brought to men sometimes by the moon and sometimes by a serpent, in other cases the serpent reveals to men the virtue that is concealed in the fruit of the moon tree or in the soma drink which can be brewed from it" (p. 53).

This last is enormously revealing in connection with the myth of the Fall. In the earlier Goddess religions, the serpent brings knowledge and healing. The moon tree supposedly grew on the moon and provided the fruit from which the soma of the gods was prepared. As Harding recounts it, an earthly soma has been brewed from a plant she identifies as "probably Asceplias Acida"—a member of the milkweed family. This wine is used in a Hindu ritual of communion. Stone (1976) identifies the tree of knowledge as the sycamore fig and notes that its flesh and fluid were used in early communion rituals of the Goddess religion. "Cretan seals and rings repeatedly depicted the Goddess or Her attendants alongside small fruit trees, caring for them, almost caressing them, as if in sacred devotion" (p. 215).

Given this history, it is not surprising that the serpent should appear as the villain in the new religion, nor that the once sacred tree of knowledge and healing should be forbidden. To destroy a religion, it is necessary to pervert its symbols and assimilate its rituals to new structures. The fifteenth verse of Genesis 3 has God declare enmity between serpent and woman, between its seed and her seed. Clearly woman is called upon to repudiate her longtime symbol of spiritual power. Paintings of the Virgin Mary crushing the head of a snake beneath her foot are for Daly (1984) "horrifyingly significant" (p. 390) because they represent women's complicity in destroying their own power. (On this, see also Phillips, 1984, and Warner, 1976.)

Teachers should not, of course, present feminist interpretations of biblical myths as the "truth" any more than they should so represent the myths themselves. It is enough to present these interpretations as a way some scholars are now looking at our religious heritage.

As women have become aware of their lost spiritual agency and power, some have understandably turned to Goddess religion. There are at least three reasons why today's students should be introduced to current literature on Goddess religion. First, the movement is intellectually, politically, and spiritually fascinating; second, its literature provides insight into the developmental possibilities of women; and third, it presents a powerful connection to current ecological interests.

In Chapter 2, I looked at the revival of interest in polytheism and the variety of definitions available to us today. Some—those suggested explicitly by William James (1902/1958) and implicitly by John Dewey (1934)—are more secular than religious and are very much alive today. But even ancient Greek polytheism is an arena of great contemporary interest. For some, the pantheon of Greek gods is a personification of universal traits and longings. The poet Auden wrote:

> To the imagination, the sacred is self-evident. It is as meaningless to ask whether one believes or disbelieves in Aphrodite or Ares as to ask whether one believes in a character in a novel; one can only say that one finds them true or untrue to life. To believe in Aphrodite and Ares merely means that one believes that the poetic myths about them do justice to the forces of sex and aggression as human beings experience them in nature and their own lives. (quoted in Downing, 1984, p. 18)

As archetypes, the gods and goddesses manifest universal developmental possibilities for both women and men. Intellectual fascination with them is revealed in literature, art, music, and many other fields. But the interest today is not merely intellectual and psychological. Carol Christ (1982) describes both political and spiritual interests. "Religion," she writes, "fulfills deep psychic needs by providing symbols and rituals that enable people to cope with limit situations in human life (death, evil, suffering) and to pass through life's important transitions (birth, sexuality, death)" (p. 72). Women need a religion in which they can find their own images in deities. "The simplest and most basic meaning of the symbol of the Goddess is the acknowledgement of the legitimacy of female power as a beneficent and independent power" (p. 75).

Part of the political interest in Goddess religion centers in fact on the notion of power. It is not necessarily the case, however, that women have more political power in a society that recognizes goddesses. Hindu society is a case in point. Almost certainly women had more freedom and power in early Hindu times, but as we shall see, this is true of many of the world's great religions. The elite versions of these traditional religions, writes David Kinsley (1989), are dominated by males, but the folk religion may reveal—as in Hinduism—Goddess worship. As we saw earlier, however, the heterodox literature may also be even more misogynist than the orthodox texts.

Goddess worship, then, cannot guarantee greater political power. It can, however, provide women with a variety of divine images by which to fashion themselves and shape their ideals. From the gentle Miao Shan of Buddhism to the fierce and beautiful Durga of Hinduism, women may find models of the best and worst in themselves and thereby come to greater understanding of themselves.

Among the genuine spiritual alternatives today is witchcraft. Here it is described by Starhawk (1982).

> In Witchcraft, each of us must reveal our own truth. Deity is seen in our own forms, whether female or male, because the Goddess has Her male aspect. Sexuality is a sacrament. Religion is a matter of relinking, with the divine within and with Her outer manifestations in all of the human and natural world. (p. 51)

I think students should be aware of today's witchcraft just as they should be aware of Eastern religions, Native American religions, humanism, and atheism. This means that they should be encouraged to approach it (if they wish) both appreciatively and critically. They should know, for example, that some of us find beauties and dangers in witchcraft surprisingly similar to those in patriarchal religion. Patriarchal religion, too, recognizes a female aspect of God, acknowledges the power of being created in God's image, and employs rituals and sacraments. Is the Goddess religion, then, as it is interpreted in witchcraft, subject to the corruptions with which we are so familiar? If not, what saves it, and cannot the same measures be taken to save traditional religion?

One of the greatest attractions of Goddess religion for today's young people is its intimate connection with the ecological movement. In this, it is similar to Native American religion and, indeed, to all nature religions (Albanese, 1991). In it, Gaia, the great Goddess, is immanent; she is in the world; she *is* the world. We are entreated to walk softly on her body and to respect all of her creatures. Starhawk (1982) writes of a Goddess who is love.

> Love of trees, of stones, of sky and clouds, of scented blossoms and thundering waves; of all that runs and flies and swims and crawls on her face; through love of ourselves; life-dissolving world-creating orgasmic love of each other; each of us unique and natural as a snowflake, each of us our own star, her Child, her lover, her beloved, her Self. (p. 56)

This passage is deeply moving, and students hearing it may feel that witches are far ahead of Baptists, Jews, and Catholics in their deep concern for harmony and peace on earth. I confess that I, too, find spirit in thundering waves (or merely lively ones in which I can frolic), in the bravery of seedlings pushing up under the mulch, in the warmth of my pet cat, in the love of my children. But similar poetic expressions can be found in the literature of the great traditional religions. The Sufis, for example, tell the following story:

> THE HEART
> Someone went up to a madman who was weeping in the bitterest possible way. He said: "Why do you cry?" The madman answered: "I am crying to attract the pity of His heart." The other told him: "Your words are nonsense, for He has no physical heart." The madman answered: "It is you who are wrong, for He is the owner of all the hearts which exist. Through the heart you can make your connections with God." (Shah, 1970, p. 63)

Our heart-to-heart connection with all living things is a pathway to God.

It is a matter of emphasis and commitment. Students must learn to ask: On what will we act? How shall we dedicate our lives? Our poetic expression and spiritual longing must be connected to a program of action in the world. What Goddess religion promises is a renewed emphasis on joyful bodily existence for all living creatures and awed respect for all creation. We will have to see whether, if it prevails, it continues to allow each individual to find his or her own image of deity and his or her own mode of communication with the divine. Conceived in the service of power, God the Mother could be as severe a tyrant as God the Father.

ALTERNATIVES THROUGH REVISION

How do the great traditional religions describe women? This is a topic of considerable interest to adolescents and, after reading feminist critiques of patriarchal religion, students will have some answers to the question. New questions can now be advanced: Have traditional religions followed their own sacred texts and early practices, or have they made choices guided by corrupt politics? Should religion be revised?

There are two main approaches to revision within the traditional religions. One concentrates on early practices and promising sections of original sacred texts; the other emphasizes the dynamic nature of faith. The second reinterprets traditional texts whereas the first points to original texts that have been ignored or underemphasized in practice. Students should be introduced to examples of both approaches.

In *Women, Religion and Sexuality* (Becher, 1990), several writers try to show that practice has departed from original intentions. Riffat Hassan (1990), for example, points to discrepancies between the Qur'an and the Hadith literature that has grown up to interpret it. Hassan argues that many of the practices that degrade women cannot be traced to the Qur'an but only to the interpretative Hadith literature. Quoting Moulvi Cheragh Ali, she writes:

> The vast flood of tradition soon formed a chaotic sea. Truth, error, fact and fable mingled together in an indistinguishable confusion. Every religious, social, and political system was defended when necessary, to please a Khalif or an Ameer to serve his purpose, by an appeal to some oral traditions. The name of Mohammed was abused to support all manner of lies and absurdities or to satisfy the passion, caprice, or arbitrary will of the despots, leaving out of consideration the creation of any standards of test. . . . I am seldom inclined to quote traditions having little or no belief in their genuineness, as generally they are inauthentic, unsupported and onesided. (p. 94)

Although she is largely in agreement with Ali, Hassan notes that elimination of the interpretive literature would in effect destroy the religious tradition. This is a subtle and important point for those intelligent believers who seek an alternative through revision. Returning to the original texts will not in itself accomplish the desired change. The interpretive literature must be amended and practice brought into line with original thought. Hence the first alternative begins to look very like the second.

Despite the difficulties, the first approach should hold special interest for educators because it demands a historical perspective on religion. Leonard Swidler (1974) affirms Hassan's claims about women's status in the Qur'an. Placing the argument in a larger context, he claims that at least some of the world's great religions started as liberation movements including both men and women.

> To the degree women later do not participate in full measure in the impulse to human liberation of a religion (i.e., sexism), that religion is unfaithful to its initial insight; it is in a state of decadence. That is, sexism is a sign of decadence in a religion. (p. 168)

Swidler (1974) goes on to document the historical decline in the status of women in Christianity, Islam, Hinduism, and Judaism. He writes: "*A return* to the original insight of these religions would tend not only to transform general religious decay to renewal, but it would also concomitantly raise the status of women in religion" (p. 168). Students may find the changes in Hindu scriptures especially dramatic. In the early scriptures, Swidler says, women were described as more nearly equal to men: "They could marry or not marry, they could study the scriptures, indeed, even devote their life to such study, they had free choice of their marriage partners, if they were widowed they could remarry, they had a right to inherit property from their fathers as well as their mothers" (p. 171).

In the later scriptures, we find horror stories that rival, and even surpass, those of Christianity. From the Pradmapurana:

> Be her husband deformed, aged, infirm, offensive in his manner; let him be choleric, debauched, immoral, a drunkard, a gambler; let him frequent places of ill-repute, live in open sin with other women, have no affection for his home; let him rave like a lunatic . . . a wife must look upon him as her god. . . . A wife must eat only after her husband has had his fill. If the latter fasts, she shall fast, too; if he touch not food, she also shall not touch it; if he be in affliction, she shall be so too; if he be cheerful, she shall share his joy. She must on the death of her husband allow herself to be burnt alive on the same funeral prye; then everybody will praise her virtue. (quoted in Swidler, 1974, pp. 173–174)

Although even well-trained scholars cannot answer the question adequately, students should be encouraged to consider the question: How and why did such deplorable changes occur in the great religions? Reflecting on such issues, intelligent believers may recognize an obligation to reform their religion by returning to its roots or by claiming a dynamism compatible with those roots. Intelligent unbelievers may find, in this story of decadence, further evidence for their contention that religion cannot lead the world to a higher level of morality.

Students should be aware, also, of how difficult the task of reform is. Reading feminists on Goddess religion or nature religion, they may be filled with a sense of spiritual renewal. But they should learn something of the struggle experienced by nineteenth century feminists in trying to move the church toward its liberatory origins. Elizabeth Cady Stanton, for example, had this to say about women and Christianity.

> A consideration of woman's position before Christianity, under Christianity, and at the present time [1888] shows that she is not indebted to any form of religion for one step of progress, nor one new liberty; on the contrary, it has been through the perversion of her religious sentiments that she has been so long held in a condition of slavery. (quoted in Oakley, 1972, p. 112)

Stanton particularly resented the choice of most preachers to emphasize Genesis 2, in which woman is created as an afterthought expressly for man, rather than Genesis 1, "which declares the full equality of the feminine and masculine element in the Godhead" (Oakley, 1972, p. 115). This choice, Stanton realized, deprived women of their image in deity. More than a hundred years ago, she urged the National Woman Suffrage Association to adopt a resolution calling "on the Christian ministry, as leaders of thought, to teach and enforce the fundamental idea of creation, that man was made in the image of God, male and female, and given equal rights over the earth, but none over each other" (Oakley, 1972, p. 114). The resolution did not pass. It was 35 years before women got the vote, and even today, in most churches, God is not addressed as Stanton recommended: "Heavenly Mother and Father." Thus it seems that the church may be harder to move than the U.S. Congress. In religion, women have collaborated in their own oppression.

Finally, it seems to me, as an educator, that profound and wonderful ideas are emerging from the work of today's feminist revisionists. They are teaching us that the body is not to be reviled and separated from theological thought (Cooey, Farmer, & Ross, 1987); that words such as "redemption" and "resurrection" should have meaning for this world as well as the next (Welch, 1985); that the tragic vision described by the early Greeks and rejected in later religious thought has tremendous power for moral life; that theodicy has long been pursuing the wrong ends.

Wendy Farley (1990) suggests a return to original stories, the parables, and brings to them a tragic vision. She writes:

> The parables are strange, provocative stories that turn heads and hearts toward a revision of historical existence. The gratuitous, passionate love of the Samaritan for his enemy or the father for his prodigal son represent real possibilities even within tragic existence. The strange logic of the parables is a logic for this world. In it widows and shepherds have the same concern for one lost coin or sheep as for the totality of their possessions; people are divided like sheep and goats on the basis of how well they cared for God incarnate in the hungry, the sick, and the criminal. It is a logic that orients human beings toward one another according to principles of justice, compassion, and celebration. It is a logic that stands over against the reality of despair, selfishness, sin, and cruelty, as a *real* alternative, not as an otherworldly consummation. It is a demand and a promise that it is possible to "do justice and love kindness" in concrete, historical life. (p. 131)

This is an inspiring passage, and I find only one major point to question. I would like students—all of us—to consider whether the parables really do direct us to *justice* or whether they turn us toward something far more fundamental. After all, was the father's treatment of the prodigal son *just*? Was the Samaritan's behavior *just*? The power of contemporary feminist criticism is that it invites us to question not only the evil in traditional thought but even its conception of good. The parable stories show us a vision of God setting aside justice in favor of responding with compassion to living needs. Students need to hear these stories and reflect on their relevance for life today.

CHAPTER 5

Immortality, Salvation, and Pessimism

Too often today students are urged to attend school and study subjects that seem irrelevant to them so that they can qualify for good jobs. Although getting a good job is a worthy aim, it is not the most important thing in life, and we underestimate teenagers when we suppose that is all that matters to them. They are in fact intensely interested in the questions we have been considering, especially those concerning life and death: Does life have any meaning? Is life worth living? Is there life after death? What does the fact of death mean for life?

DEATH

Students should have opportunities to discuss death and its connection to the meaning of life. In Chapter 1, I discussed John Silber's (1989) recommendation that children be exposed "to what is true, to a confrontation with what is real" (p. 5). He believes that a recognition of death's reality will encourage students to work harder and to live more morally. In opposition to Silber, I believe that students must be helped to find meaning and joy in life—that many definitions of success should be available to them. I also believe that love and care play a greater role than fear in developing moral attitudes and behaviors. Death should indeed be discussed but in connection with life and its meaning.

Children and adolescents worry periodically about death. In a recent newspaper column, Adair Lara (1992) described her son Patrick's anger over the fact of death. One night at bedtime, his brooding led to a brief confrontation.

"You made me die," he said, when all I was doing was trying to get him to brush his teeth. "I gave you life," I answered. "Yes," he answered bitterly, "so I can die."

These bitter moments pass in healthy relationships, but the need to discuss existential questions continues. On the same day that the Lara column appeared, the comic strip Calvin and Hobbes contained a similar episode. Calvin's teacher was preparing the class to move on to a new unit of work.

Teacher: If there are no questions, we'll move on to the next chapter.
Calvin: I have a question.
Teacher: Certainly, Calvin. What is it?
Calvin: What's the point of human existence?
Teacher: I meant any questions about the subject at hand.
Calvin: Oh. (Staring at his book, he mumbles, "Frankly, I'd like to have the issue resolved before I expend any more energy on this.")

Now, of course, very few kids ask such questions point-blank as Calvin did. But they wonder, and worry, and wish for adults to respond to questions asked and unasked. It *is* hard to concentrate on English grammar or long division when you're thinking about the point of life itself.

Death can be discussed in a historical context. Philippe Aries (1981) begins his monumental history of death with an analysis of attitudes toward death in the Middle Ages. As students read of Roland and Oliver, of King Arthur, of Tristan, their attention can be drawn to the attitude of these men toward death. First, Aries points out, they saw that death was coming and prepared for it. While their companions grieved and sometimes protested, they accepted their own deaths. Foreknowledge of death was as certain as vivid memories of the past.

Gradually, this close connection between the natural and what we today call the supernatural gave way, and a great gap appeared between "the people" and intellectuals. Aries (1981) writes:

After the split that divided the *literati* from traditional culture, presentiments of death were ranked with popular superstitions, even by writers who regarded them as poetic and venerable. Nothing could be more significant of this than the way Chateaubriand speaks of them in *Le Genie du Christianisme*, as a charming example of folklore: "Death so poetic because it touches on the immortal, so mysterious because of its silence, had a thousand ways of making its presence known," but he adds, *"for the people."* It would be impossible to admit more openly that the educated classes no longer perceived the premonitory signs of death. . . . For Chateaubriand, the "thousand ways . . . " are all supernatural: "Sometimes death announced its presence by the tolling of a bell that rang all by itself; sometimes the man who was about to die heard three knocks on the floor of his room." (p. 8)

Today we do not know whether "the people" retained a closer connection to nature and their own bodily processes or whether, as Chateaubriand suggests, they were merely victims of superstition. However, there are people even today—many Native Americans, for example—who maintain a serene attitude toward impending death. Forewarnings, such as the owl calling one's name, are received with composure and trigger ceremonial preparation rather than terror and resistance.

Ritual acceptance of death is also illustrated in the medieval mysteries of Ellis Peters whose Brother Cadfael solved murder mysteries in the twelfth century. These stories are both fun to read and historically informative. The bits of ordinary life are especially interesting. The dependence on order, the comfort of ritual, the serenity induced by ceremony, the stability of good character are all depicted in fiction just as Aries describes them historically.

It might be helpful, also, for young people to learn that—for all the serenity with which normal death was accepted—sudden death, especially murder, was reviled in the Middle Ages. It was not only that the victim and his loved ones had no opportunity to prepare but, worse, that such a death was an affront to order. It disrupted the sense of destiny and human knowledge of destiny. People who would normally mourn overtly and communally fell peculiarly silent when such deaths occurred (Aries, 1981, p. 11).

Surely students should be allowed to discuss the present epidemic of violent death among the young. There is nothing heroic or romantic or serene about dying from bullet wounds on one's own doorstep. This is neither a brave warrior's death nor the natural death of the aged. Sometimes young people who reject appeals to justice and what is morally right finally see the horror of their participation in gang activity when someone bereaved by their acts describes what those acts have meant for the ordinary lives of loved ones. These descriptions remain as vivid today as they were in the Middle Ages. Sudden, nonparticipatory, death is seen as a violation of the natural order, an intrusion into the legitimate plans and expectations of people who had reason to anticipate a different destiny. Sitting on one's doorstep, strolling on the sidewalk, chatting with neighbors, one should be safe to plan one's next moments and days. It is not law and order in the civil sense that appeals to us here. It is natural order. Even if, in our intellectual sophistication, we reject such a notion, we cannot deny its power to influence many people who have little regard for civil order. The sense of having disrupted lives that were destined for alternative experience can be a powerful influence.

Here, again, we see that history, literature, and multicultural perspectives can be brought to bear on topics of central human interest. Instead of depending on standard history and literature to handle the great existential questions—where those questions are often lost in a welter of facts and technical analyses—educators should plan curriculum to address the questions directly and teach history and literature as they contribute to the larger enterprise.

But as we discuss death and the attitudes people have taken toward it, we must also discuss immortality and the variety of perspectives people have developed on that subject. Is death the end of life or the beginning of a new existence? Is the life we experience now merely the most recent in a long chain of existences?

IMMORTALITY

Every human being seems to have wondered about the possibility of life after death. Even those convinced for or against immortality confess occasional doubt. Miguel De Unamuno (1954) has described the doubts on both sides. Persuaded of the finality and desirability of death, an unbeliever may nonetheless hear an inner voice murmur, "Who knows!" Similarly, the confessed believer may be disquieted by the same inner whisper, "Who knows?" Unamuno goes on to say:

> "Is there?" "Is there not?"—these are the bases of our inner life. There may be a rationalist who has never wavered in his conviction of the mortality of the soul, and there may be a vitalist who has never wavered in his faith in immortality; but at the most this would only prove that just as there are natural monstrosities, so there are those who are stupid as regards heart and feeling, however great their intelligence, and those who are stupid intellectually, however great their virtue. . . . I do not understand those men who tell me that the prospect of the yonder side of death has never tormented them, that the thought of their own death never disquiets them. (p. 119)

Martin Gardner (1983) agrees with Unamuno that there is no way for a rationalist to prove either immortality or mortality—that the passion of desire and conviction sustain believers. He has little patience with what he calls "pseudo-immortalities"—those concocted by "atheists and pantheists." Gardner, like Unamuno, wants a continuation of himself—his personality, memories, full consciousness.

However, the pseudo-immortalities might appeal to some readers, and students should hear about them. How about living on through our descendants? Condemned men on California's death row have recently brought suit to allow exactly this kind of immortality for themselves. They want to contribute to sperm banks so that their genes will live on. Other people foresee a satisfactory immortality in works of art, buildings, political organizations, or other tangible things they have created. When I listen to Beethoven's Emperor Concerto, I feel the immortality of Beethoven. But would this form of immortality content Beethoven the man? Still others find comfort in the physical fact that their atoms will be redistributed in other living and nonliving things. Gardner (1983) found this not in the least comforting. "In that sense of immortality," he wrote, "every blade of grass, every pebble, every snowflake is immortal" (p. 281). Some of us *do* want our bodies to nourish the earth, not to be sealed away from it in an incorruptible coffin, but even so, many who feel this way would prefer that their souls or consciousness could observe the resulting bloom of life and move on to see, to feel, to love, and to live again.

Gardner was especially hard on philosophers who try to convince us that our immortality consists in our forever being exactly what we have been—a sort of permanent record in the universe. This is the kind of comfort sometimes offered to parents of those who die young: The deceased child will be forever young. In this version, the doctrine is heartless. But in others it has a certain compensatory plausibility. Each of us becomes a memory—a complete, accurate memory—in the mind of God. "God" here is not, of course, a personal God who responds to us as individuals. While labeling this view pompous and shameful, Gardner (1983) acknowledges that some sensitive philosophers have held it. Santayana, for example, "was honest enough to say that in spite of its stoic compensations the view has beneath it an 'incurable sorrow'" (p. 281).

The view just described has been common in the process theology mentioned in Chapter 2. (Santayana and Whitehead, both named by Gardner, belonged to this tradition.) It is called "objective immortality" because, although the individual subjective consciousness is not preserved, an eternal record becomes part of God's experience. At least some contemporary process theologians admit that this view strikes most people as inadequate. (See Griffin, 1991.) Selfish or not, most people want their own experience to continue. They are not content with a tiny contribution to the divine experience.

Gardner (1983) was at his literary best when he rejected all these views together with one that found solace in the eternal persistence of Truth.

> It does not fortify *my* soul in the least to know that after I die all unmarried men will still be bachelors, that 37 will still be a prime number, that the stars will continue to shine, and that forever I will have been just what I am now. Away with these fake immortalities! They mean nothing to the heart. Better to say with Bertrand Russell: "I believe that when I die I shall rot, and nothing of my ego will survive." (p. 282)

Even though Gardner himself rejected atheism, Russell's statement had a ring of honesty for him, and this illustrates again how close believers and unbelievers can be when they share their deepest concerns.

The paragraph from Gardner also illustrates how rich discussion can be in a math class. The reference to bachelors as unmarried men is, of course, one of the best-known analytic statements in philosophy; the one to 37 as a prime number reflects Gardner's central interest in mathematics. A mathematics teacher might, for example, ask: If 37 is written as a numeral in base 5 (122_5) is it still a prime number? (The answer is yes, but the question challenges students' understanding of the concept of primeness.) Both of Gardner's chapters on immortality are filled with references to literature, philosophy, science fiction, mathematics, theology, and poetry. If mathematics teachers could get past the idea that their sole job is to teach mathematics, school might be a far more interesting place for students.

Immortality has been defined in many ways. The nature religion of Native Americans in colonial new England was described by both Roger Williams and William Wood as very like that of the Turks. Wood wrote:

> They hold [of] the immortality of the never-dying soul that it shall pass to the southwest Elysium, concerning which their Indian faith jumps much with the Turkish Alcoran, holding it to be a kind of paradise wherein they shall everlastingly abide, solacing themselves in odiferous gardens, fruitful corn fields, green meadows, bathing their tawny hides

in the cool streams of pleasant rivers, and shelter themselves from heat and cold in the sumptuous palaces framed by the skill of nature's curious contrivement: concluding that neither care nor pain shall molest them. (quoted in Albanese, 1991, p. 33)

Other peoples have put as much emphasis on pre-existence as on afterlife. Some Eastern European Jews believed that every soul exists from creation and that memory of this existence is wiped out by a slap just before birth (Mead, 1961). Plato (and, perhaps, Socrates), too, put considerable emphasis on immortality in the sense of pre-existence. For him, all knowledge was essentially recall from the vast storage of eternity.

Margaret Mead (1961) described a form of Indonesian Hinduism practiced by the Balinese. Believing in reincarnation, the Balinese attribute much of good or ill fortune to past incarnations.

A long run of bad luck may be blamed on debts that one of one's souls contracted during its stay in the other world, and people will say, "I am having bad luck this incarnation." Or, in giving to a beggar, they may remark, "I would not dare not to give to him. Who knows when I may not be as he? We all take turns." (p. 92)

In Bali, the veil of ignorance (Rawls, 1971)—which is for us a mere technical device in moral philosophy—is a fact of existence! One literally does not know one's position in the next incarnation.

For some, then, immortality is forward-looking, for others backward-looking. For some, it is something to be heartily desired and sought after; for others, it is something to be rid of through the elimination of all desires. Some believe that the souls of the dead dwell in a special place; others, that they remain nearby to visit good or ill on the living; still others, that they must be got rid of because they are essentially evil. Sometimes mixtures of these views exist in wild contradiction. In Chapter 3, we heard a priest observe that his parishioners believed three things simultaneously: the Church's teachings on immortality; that when you're dead you're dead—just like an animal; and that the dead from under the ground continue to watch the living malevolently.

There is at least one more view of immortality that should be mentioned here. Some thinkers have held that a form of immortality can be achieved by transcending time during one's own lifetime (Heard, 1961). This remarkable feat is accomplished by engaging so totally with an object of study or contemplation that one passes beyond ordinary temporal events. Several great mathematicians have described such intervals in their own lives, and observers have written accounts of their behavior at such times. Heard (1961) cited Descartes, Newton, Hamilton, and Poincaré as outstanding cases. All of these men seemed capable of achieving a remarkable state of nonsensory awareness. Newton often entered trance-like states and had to be led into the dining hall. E. T. Bell (1937/1965) wrote of him:

> Never careful of his bodily health, Newton seems to have forgotten that he had a body which required food and sleep when he gave himself up to the composition of his masterpiece [*Mathematical Principles of Natural Philosophy*]. Meals were ignored or forgotten, and on arising from a snatch of sleep he would sit on the edge of the bed half-clothed for hours, threading the mazes of his mathematics. (p. 109)

Newton, apparently, lived partly in this world and partly in another. Hamilton, too, was described as neglecting food (but not alcohol!) and ordinary activities for days at a time, returning to everyday life with wonderful mathematical insights. Descartes said that he did his best work in the barely awakened state first thing in the morning and often remained in bed thinking. Poincaré (1956) wrote a fascinating essay, "Mathematical Creation," describing in detail the role of incubation in mathematical activity. Of the four, only Poincaré was an avowed religious skeptic, and Newton considered theology more important than mathematics. However, it is questionable whether any of them would have described their capacities for nonsensory awareness as a form of immortality.

Mathematicians are not the only creative people to experience moods in which they are seized by their objects of study. Mozart insisted that, when conditions were favorable, he "heard" music in his head, and Tennyson seems actually to have cultivated the state of nonsensory awareness. Indeed, Tennyson explicitly connected this state with immortality, saying that—having experienced it—he knew that death was a "laughable impossibility" (Heard, 1961, p. 69). This is not to say, however, that Tennyson equated the state with immortality but that, from it, he understood the nature and certainty of immortality.

In all likelihood, both Gardner and Unamuno would reject this transcendent mental state (which is, after all, temporary and dependent on a high order of mental activity) as another pseudo-immortality. How might high school students react? Some would probably say that, far from being periodically immortal, "these guys might as well have been dead!" But surely some would see the mystical beauty in such engagement.

Before leaving this topic, we should note that great religious figures—Paul and Augustine come to mind—have also described themselves as seized by a greater power. Neither, however, saw these moments as a substitute for the immortality that Gardner and Unamuno sought. Others have seen the capacity for engaging in such activity—for entering such exalted mental states—as a merit deserving immortality. It is not just the *name* of a great artist that must be preserved, not just his or her works, but the very *self* with whom later thinkers must converse. This seems to be the view held by Vladimir Nabokov, who tried desperately to connect literary and personal immortality. (See Rorty, 1989.) Nabokov, much to his credit, saw the difficulty in this view. It is highly elitist. Preserving great artists and scientists so that their conversations can continue is lovely for them, but what about the rest of humankind? Nevertheless, Nabokov believed in immortality, even if he could *justify* it only for part of humanity: "We believe ourselves to be mortal just as the madman believes himself to be God," he had one of his characters say (quoted in Rorty, 1989, p. 146). The argument from artistic sensibility cannot produce—not logically at any rate—such conviction, but Nabokov felt the need to voice such a belief through an invented character.

Frederick Turner (1991) also comments on this view, holding that our immortality consists of participation in eternal conversations.

> So the heart of the immortality of the great conversation lies outside the conventional objects, skills, traditions, and expertise of discourse. It is not . . . merely immortality for the Great Minds; for it is precisely when these great minds give up being great minds—being experts, authorities, professionals—and become amateurs, laypersons—bullshitters, if you like—that they become immortal. Socrates and company jumped all the fences, like sophomores. (p. 107)

From this perspective, we invite students to share in a form of immortality when we engage them in the kind of discussions we have been considering.

So far, except for a brief reference to Russell's belief that, upon death, he would "rot," I have said nothing of the unbeliever's view, and most of this I will save for the section on pessimism and Chapter 6 on humanism. But I should note here that a belief in immortality is not always a result of religious belief. Some philosophers have argued for immortality on the basis of nontheistic metaphysical premises, and others have grounded their belief in parapsychology. Arguments from both arenas might interest students.

SALVATION

The views on immortality most familiar to high school students are probably those associated with salvation. Christians derive their faith in immortality from the Resurrection, and no other religious concept calls forth greater emphasis on belief. In Protestant Christianity especially, one's salvation depends entirely on belief in Jesus Christ as the risen savior. Speaking for all Christians, Hans Kung (1990) writes:

> The unconditionally reliable reality, to which men and women can hold fast for all time and eternity, is not the Bible texts and not the Fathers of the Church, nor the Church's magisterium, but *God himself, as he spoke for believers through Jesus Christ.* The texts of the Bible, the sayings of the Fathers and church authorities mean to be—with varying degrees of importance—no more and no less than an expression of this belief. (p. 62)

This is, perhaps, the hardest topic for teachers to discuss with public school students. For teachers who are committed Christians it would be especially hard because belief in Jesus as savior is bound up with truth and personal salvation. A committed Christian cannot say simply that this is *a* belief; it is necessarily *his* or *her* belief. Yet it may be possible for well-educated Christian teachers to discuss the idea of salvation in a broader context and to acknowledge other views. For all students, discussion of the Christian concept is essential in understanding evangelicism. Those who believe that there is one and only one path to salvation feel themselves duty-bound to point others to that path, and their persistence can be understood, if not welcomed, when we recognize their beliefs. At the same time, students should be helped to understand how inconsiderate the evangelical stance can be. Martin Buber (1967) described the pain he suffered as a schoolboy in Christian classrooms. That experience gave him a lifelong aversion to all missionary activity directed at people who already had their own beliefs. Understanding why people engage in evangelical activity helps us look on them with compassion, but it does not necessarily lead us to agree with or admire their choice.

It should be helpful to all students to learn that the notions of salvation and saviors appear in other religions.

> The saviour is an essential figure in religion, because many religious people are convinced that the domain of men and the world of the gods are separated by a deep cleft. In order to link up these two worlds a bridge must be laid across the cleft. Man is unable to perform this act. It should be done by a creature who unites the two worlds by his nature. That is the saviour. (Bleeker, 1963, p. 2)

The world's great religions have very different expectations of their savior gods. In some, such as Christianity, the savior is unique; in others, as in Buddhism, saviors are multiplied as more and more people move toward enlightenment. Immortality—the gift of continued life—is the gift of some saviors; others intervene in this world to save supplicants from ill fortune or danger. In some religions, the savior is divine from the outset; in others, something like divinity is achieved by the continuous earthly struggle for enlightenment.

In its great interest in life after death, the ancient Egyptian religion bears many resemblances to Christianity. When Isis and her sister mourners sing, "Raise thyself, thou art risen, thou shalt not die, thine soul will live. . . . Thou dost triumph, O Osiris, king of the dead" (Bleeker, 1963, p. 8), the sentiment sounds familiar to modern Christians. But in the Egyptian tale, it is Isis, a goddess, who served as savior, and eventually—by the Hellenistic period—she played the role of redeemer for individuals who called upon her. In another similarity to Christianity, Isis apparently required confession and penance from her followers. But, of course, neither Isis nor Osiris was claimed as the one and only deity. Finally, the rites of ritual assimilation in the Osirian religion and Christianity are strikingly similar. (See Brandon, 1963, pp. 32–33.) In both religions, assimilation to the risen savior is symbolized in ceremonial ritual.

In contrast, the savior-gods of Buddhism have little to do with life after death or the forgiveness of sins. In Chinese Buddhism, for example, we find the beautiful story of Kuan-yin who sacrificed her own life (as the princess Miao Shan) to help others and to achieve spiritual purity. In the legend, Miao Shan even descends into hell and transforms it into a paradise! (Kinsley, 1989, p. 32). Because her great compassion threatens to ruin hell, she is sent back to the living. Kinsley writes:

> There is no doubt that the central role of Kuan-yin is that of helper and savior. In this respect, she quite clearly conforms to the traditional role of the bodhissattva in Mahayana Buddhism. A bodhissattva is a being destined for full enlightenment and *nirvana* who, out of compassion for the suffering of other beings, has taken a vow to postpone his or her entry into *nirvana* in order to remain in the world to help other beings. (p. 35)

Kuan-yin is a deity who listens to and attends to the world's sufferers. It is believed that she intervenes miraculously for those in danger who call upon her. As Kinsley (1989) describes her,

> Kuan-yin's appeal lies in the fact that she hearkens to her devotees' pleas for help in *this* world. While other Buddhist figures, such as Amitabha, appeal primarily to the devotees' desire for rebirth in heaven after death, or to the desire for enlightenment and subsequent release from the world of human suffering, Kuan-yin's compassionate actions often focus on life in this world. (p. 40)

But Kuan-yin plays another role that is potentially significant in spiritual education. For one thing, she represents the compassionate side of deity. Kuan-yin first appeared as male but, gradually, came to be seen as female. Further, she serves as a bridge between Buddhism and Confucianism. In her filial piety (she sacrifices her arms and eyes to save her father, who has treated her badly) and compassion for suffering in daily life, she exhibits the finest Confucian virtues. In her rejection of riches and material comfort, she is clearly Buddhist. Teachers and students who read the legends of Kuan-yin may come to a deep appreciation of the Chinese genius for religious tolerance and synthesis.

There is a strong humanistic trend in Confucianism that suggests another slant on salvation. D. Howard Smith (1963) writes:

> After the time of Confucius, salvation, conceived of in terms of an ordered society, a good life here and now, and freedom from suffering and evil, was thought of as achievable by human effort alone; but only through conformity with the cosmic law which pervades the universe. . . . Even in Mo-Tzu, though T'ien loves the people and seeks their happiness and well-being, there is no thought of T'ien's saving grace. Salvation is the result of human effort as man models himself on T'ien and seeks to do the will of T'ien. (p. 177)

Kuan-yin also bears a resemblance to Taoist sages and symbolizes a state of perfection in this world. Hence followers may strive to be like her and, in a sense, to share in her perfection. Discussion of salvation in the context of the Kuan-yin legends may, thus, lead to several desirable outcomes: realization that salvation is not exclusively a Christian concept, admiration for a beautiful and inspiring religious figure, broadened cultural understanding, appreciation for Chinese religious thought, a deeper sympathy for polytheistic perspectives, and an awakened interest in feminine aspects of the divine.

In the Hindu religions, too, a female deity is associated with salvation. Laksmi both creates and destroys; like Kuan-yin, she responds to petitioners and bestows good fortune. In describing herself, she sounds somewhat like the Jewish deity.

> I alone send (the creation) forth and (again) destroy it. I absolve the sins of the good. As the (mother) earth towards all beings, I pardon them (all their sins). I mete everything out. I am the thinking process and I am contained in everything. (Kinsley, 1989, p. 66—from the Laksmi Tantra)

Laksmi is a deity in her own right even though her powers are delegated by Visnu. She is the one who listens and responds. But, although female deities may grant salvation, mortal women are dependent on their husbands for salvation. The goddess Sita represents the ideal wife. Her husband, Rama, is her god, and she finds her life meaningless without him.

> For a woman, it is not her father, her son, nor her mother, friends nor own self, but the husband, who in this world and the next is ever her sole means of salvation. (Kinsley, 1989, p. 98)

Throughout the discussion of salvation, students may detect the confluence of religion and politics: Kuan-yin as a symbol of reconciliation among competing traditions, Laksmi and Sita as exemplars of the good wife and the power accorded those who accept their proper position, even Mary, the mother of Jesus, whose power derives from her obedience. Mary has been and continues to be an attractive figure in Catholic Christianity, and the Church has had to control her power by denying her divinity. Yet Catholics all over the world call upon her in time of trouble to intercede with her son and soften his judgment. Like Kuan-yin and Laksmi, she is seen as compassionate and responsive—a key figure in the quest for salvation.

Another conception of the savior-god appears in Judaism. Here God acts not as a bridge between earth and heaven, nor as one of a host of intercessors in individual lives, but as the savior of a people. In contrast to Christianity, salvation is not so dependent on belief as on right action with respect to both God and human beings. The coming of the kingdom has to be earned by collective obedience. The early Jewish conception of salvation was clearly one of salvation in this world and one in which human beings were called upon to play a significant role. Later Jewish conceptions involved resurrection, but this notion differs from the idea of an immortal soul that escapes a decaying body. Usually it involves a fresh act of creation on the part of God; the body is recreated and, again, mortal goodness contributes to God's decision whether or not to resurrect a given person.

Judaism reflects the influence of other religions in its various outlooks on salvation. In addition to the early, and continuously influential, idea of salvation on this earth and the later notion of resurrection at the final judgment, many Jews have adopted the Platonic view of the soul's immortality.

> Thus, the Pittsburgh Platform of Reform Judaism stated: "We reassert the doctrine of Judaism that the soul is immortal. . . . We reject as ideas not rooted in Judaism the beliefs both in bodily resurrection and in Gehanna and Eden (Hell and Paradise) as abodes of everlasting punishment or reward." (Braunthal, 1979, p. 103)

For many students, discussion of death, immortality, and salvation will lead to greater appreciation of their own religious views. For others, recognition of the historical antecedents of their traditions and the universality of savior stories will lead to doubt and, perhaps, to humanism. For a good many—both believers and unbelievers—such discussion may lead to depression and even morbidity. We turn next, therefore, to a consideration of pessimism.

PESSIMISM

Why discuss pessimism with high school students? One obvious reason mentioned in Chapter 1 is that teenagers are, like everyone else, subject to moods of depression, but they are often unaware how acutely even wise and successful adults also suffer from it. A second reason is that much of humanity's compassion, courage, and wisdom has developed out of pessimism. A third reason is that some high

school students today live almost continuously in the dangerous grip
of gloom. Fascinated by cruelty and violence, they flirt with suicide,
or they are tempted to fight their own fear by inflicting pain on
others. So we have ample reasons for exploring the topic with teenagers.

Students may be surprised to learn that they are not the world's
first pessimists, and they may be astonished to hear that pessimism
is thought by many to be a product of religious longing. Speaking to
college students, William James (1899) said, "Pessimism is essentially
a religious disease. In the form of it to which you are most liable, it
consists in nothing but a religious demand to which there comes no
normal religious reply" (p. 39).

James thought that those attracted to nature religions were most
subject to this form of pessimism. If, that is, people locate God in
nature, they are bound to see evil as well as glory everywhere. Nature
simply cannot manifest accurately the God of love and mercy sought
by the religious heart. "Here on our very hearts and in our gardens,"
wrote James (1902/1958), "the infernal cat plays with the panting
mouse, or holds the hot bird fluttering in her jaws." Further, "The
normal process of life contains moments as bad as any of those which
insane melancholy is filled with, moments in which radical evil gets
its innings and takes its turn. The lunatic's visions of horror are all
drawn from the material of daily fact. Our civilization is founded on
the shambles, and every individual existence goes out in a lonely
spasm of helpless agony" (p. 138). Even teenagers might have a hard
time exceeding the gloom described by James.

Those who adopt a Christian view of salvation can often escape
this gloom, but even many committed Christians cannot overcome it
entirely, and, like Unamuno, they take a tragic view of life. Other
religions reject the very idea of personal salvation or a personal savior. In Buddhism, for example, the religious goal is not the continu-
ance of personal consciousness in paradise but escape from the inevitable longings, pains, and desires of conscious existence.

Schopenhauer's pessimism had an Eastern cast. Describing the
world as Will, Schopenhauer found it totally evil because the will to
live—the very element that constitutes the living world—is always
and inexorably thwarted. What kind of God would create such a
world? asked Schopenhauer. Only a God who is evil, indifferent, or
careless. Schopenhauer (1893/1976) found an attractive answer to the
charge of God's carelessness in Eastern religion: "Brahma is said to
have produced the world by a kind of fall or mistake; and in order to
atone for his folly, he is bound to remain in it himself until he works

out his redemption. As an account of the origin of things, that is admirable!'' (p. 22). Nietzsche found the Greek gods admirable on the same grounds—that they shared human foibles and pains. And, of course, there is a long tradition in Judaism and Christianity of the suffering God, but Christians have not been willing to trace suffering to God's agency, and often they have even rejected the possibility of a perfect God's suffering.

Students may be smart enough to ask where this suffering God or Brahma *is*. They do not see or feel such a presence. At this point, we encounter all the problems discussed earlier on the silence of God. But if they are willing to follow Schopenhauer a bit farther, they may at least question suicide as a remedy for life's suffering. Like many serious pessimists, Schopenhauer saw that the only logical response to a totally senseless life-world was to reject life outright. Suicide, yes, but not suicide as we usually think of it. What we must do, Schopenhauer advised, was to overcome all will and desire. Physically killing ourselves is *not* the answer because the act itself shows that we still desire a solution or remedy. Instead we must give up all desires and all willing. But, students may ask, how do we give up willing? Surely not by willing ourselves to stop willing! Further, most of us are unwilling to give up even our temporary joys for the sake of a universe free from desire and will. Schopenhauer, they may decide, asks too much of us.

We could, of course, return to questions concerning the nature of God and what kind of God would create such a world, but let's put that aside for now and concentrate on the issue of our own pessimism. If Schopenhauer's answer—or that of the Buddhists—does not appeal to us, what else can we do?

James answered with two possibilities: We can give up the search for a religious response from the universe or we can deepen our religious intelligence. The first requires us to give up the idea that God—if there is a God—will respond to humans through the natural world. James (1899) quotes Carlyle taking himself to task through his character Teufelsdrockh in *Sartor Resartus*.

"Wherefore, like a coward, dost thou forever pip and whimper, and go cowering and trembling? Despicable biped! . . . Hast thou not a heart; canst thou not suffer whatsoever it be . . . ? Let it come, then; I will meet it and defy it!'' (pp. 44–45)

Carlyle's character had decided to protest against the injustice of the universe, and he shouted at the Devil, "I am not thine, but Free, and forever hate thee!'' ''From that hour,'' he says, ''I began to be a man'' (pp. 44–45). He was, temporarily at least, free of both good and evil spirits.

This kind of response, as James says, is a rebellion against a God—good or evil—supposed to be responsible for the affairs of human beings. Rejecting such a God enables some of us to fight finite evils and to pursue ordinary pleasures without guilt. An important point arises here, and it may appeal to many teenagers. A pessimistic world view does not have to lead to indifference, despair, or cruelty. On the contrary, it can lead to an ethic of compassion (as Schopenhauer insisted) and a life filled with moments of intense joy (as Unamuno saw so clearly). Indeed, optimism seems more often than pessimism to lead to cruelty. Consider how easily Leibniz accepted the suffering in this ''best of all possible worlds.'' The pessimist who rejects Spirit as the source or allayer of suffering often takes up a courageous human responsibility to relieve suffering and overcome injustice. Thus pessimists who become unbelievers may subdue their pessimism and live active lives of surpassing goodness.

The other solution discussed by James is to deepen our religious intelligence. For James this meant growing beyond nature religions—giving up the notion that this world, or this universe, is a total or adequate manifestation of God. From this perspective, one must trust—must have faith—that there is something beyond the sensible universe that justifies the life we see and live. Just living by this trust may indeed provide a justification for it. Believing that life is worth living, and living as though the belief were true, can make it so.

Now, oddly, when I read James, I find his first—irreligious—solution to pessimism more religious than his second. The second, which, for James at least, amounted to a faith that even horrible things might work in the end for the greatest good, slides over into the optimism of theodicy—an optimism that many of us fear more than pessimism. James (1899) describes a story he heard as a medical student: If the suffering dog strapped to a board undergoing vivisection—screaming his pain and fear—could understand the purposes served by his suffering, he might summon the courage to endure and even take pride in his sacrifice. Here, it seems to me, James comes perilously close to Augustine and Leibniz, and I would rather cast my lot with those who accept their lonely responsibility to relieve suffering and avoid its infliction. If the dog's suffering is not absolutely essential (and it rarely is), relieve it! Unstrap and quit torturing the poor animal! Rarely can an abstract ''good for all'' justify the deliberate infliction of pain on an individual who will not profit from that good.

But there are more persuasive and touching accounts of deepening religious intelligence and feeling. Arthur Miller (1987) is often described as a pessimist, although he rejects the label. He has also said that he doesn't recommend teaching children religion because "too often God is death and it is death that is being worshipped and 'loved'" (p. 26)—and this is the point with which I started this chapter—but his religious sensitivity is clearly acute. He says that "God certainly is always about to exist" (p. 559) and that "in some primal layer, Law is God's thought" (p. 584)—a characteristically traditional Jewish thought. But more touching than these occasional nods to God are his childhood memories of visits to the synagogue with his great-grandfather. One late afternoon after they had prayed in the synagogue, his great-grandfather instructed him to close his eyes. Great-grandfather took off his shoes, raised his prayer shawl over his head, and moved toward a group of other old men. Miller, just a small child, heard singing, and he could not resist peeking.

> My rising fear separated two fingers over one eye, and I peeked through the fuzz of eyelashes and saw the most astonishing thing—about fifteen old men, bent over and covered completely by their prayer shawls, all of them in white socks, *dancing*! (p. 39)

Miller wondered then why he had been told to cover his eyes. What was forbidden? Their lack of shoes, or dignity, or just that "they were being happy even though they were old"? "For I had never heard a music like this," writes Miller, "so wild and crazy, and each man dancing without any relation to another but only toward the outer darkness that enveloped the spaces beyond family and men, the spaces you might say listened to prayers" (p. 39).

This account seems to me to illustrate a deepening of religious intelligence and feeling. It is more trustworthy somehow than James's suggestion of some great good that can justify the horrors we see and hear about daily. But the first way, to quit asking of God and the universe what they cannot give, is also attractive. So which attitude is more religious? We may not be able to answer this. Certainly many people have derived courage and joy from the belief that, behind the world's surface manifestations of pain, a great God intends eventual good. Others raise a fist of defiance to any Spirit who would create or teach through pain. They intend to show by their own lives that things need not be ordered by such cruelty. Many believers hang onto their faith while nevertheless embracing pessimism with respect to this world. Many unbelievers rid themselves of both pessimism and faith in one and the same act of rejection. Deep inside, however, unbelievers may suspect that somewhere, somehow, their compassionate defiance is exactly what some benevolent God wants, and Unamuno's inner voice still whispers, "Who knows, who knows?"

CHAPTER 6

Humanism and Unbelief

The discussion of pessimism disclosed a way of thinking about spirituality and morality that does not depend on belief in deities—at least, not on deities who intervene in the world of human affairs. If people give up belief in gods, what beliefs guide their lives?

HISTORICAL HUMANISM

The foundations of modern humanism were laid by Desiderius Erasmus and Giovanni Pico della Mirandola. Both writers broke with the predestinarian tradition of church thought (as had some Medieval thinkers before them) and put great emphasis on the role of humans in determining their own fortunes. Pico stressed human dignity, and Erasmus emphasized freedom of will and reason (Braunthal, 1979). Humanism, as these men began to define it, seeks the perfection of humankind through its own efforts. Some humanists are religious humanists (as Erasmus was), and for them humanism merely has a different emphasis—one that does not depend on salvation solely through grace. But many humanists break with god-religions entirely and adopt a belief in human effort and progress. In recent decades, the almost eschatological faith of humanists in progress has faded, but this loss of faith, one might argue, has not weakened humanism. On the contrary, accepting as a fact that progress is not guaranteed, makes human reason, effort, and devotion all the more important.

If pessimism is, as James described it, a religious disease, a vigorous humanism is one of its cures. Bertrand Russell described himself this way.

> Three passions, simple but overwhelmingly strong, have governed my life: the longing for love, the search for knowledge, and unbearable pity for the suffering of mankind. (quoted in Ruland, 1985, p. 107)

This combination of passions led Russell to a life of extraordinary activism on behalf of social causes and continual analysis of both humanist and religious positions.

Russell is an outstanding model for inquiring students. Accepting humanism as an alternative to religion, he nevertheless remained wary of humanist positions that smacked of dogma. Vernon Ruland (1985) writes of Russell's passions and insistence on the modest place of humans in the universe.

> Moreover, human nature must not be viewed as separable from the unfathomable, numinous matrix of cosmic Nature within which it is only one evolving component. Responding to a questionnaire once sent him by *Humanist* magazine, Russell hesitated to identify himself with the Humanist tag used by this organization because he had been finding "the nonhuman part of the cosmos . . . much more interesting and satisfactory than the human part." (p. 108)

In this time of environmentalism—when even some scientists are entertaining the Gaia hypothesis—Russell's comments may have special impact.

People become humanists for a variety of reasons. Some retain religious connections but linger on the edge of heresy. Some cannot believe what religions teach; of these, some—like Martin Gardner—forsake institutional religion but remain committed theists. Some never consider religion seriously, regarding it as nonsense from start to finish. Still others—and these seem to be the people James referred to as suffering a religious disease—look conscientiously at religion and find it not only disappointing but harmful. Students should be acquainted with all of these views, but especially the last.

INTELLECTUAL OBJECTIONS TO RELIGION

In the first five chapters, we have already encountered many objections to religion. Among the strongest are moral objections: persecution and cruelty, prohibitions on the free exercise of reason and inquiry, convoluted arguments about the nature of gods, subordination of women, and (in Christianity) the hamstringing of life with a doctrine of sin and the exploitation of nonhuman life and natural resources.

In Chapter 3, Bertrand Russell (1963) was quoted as saying that religion "sanctified" our base and cruel passions. Further, he wrote:

> I think all of the great religions of the world—Buddhism, Hinduism, Christianity, Islam, and Communism—both untrue and harmful. . . . What the world needs is not dogma but an attitude of scientific inquiry combined with a belief that the torture of millions is not desirable, whether inflicted by Stalin or by a Deity imagined in the likeness of the believer. (p. 203)

Ruland (1985) comments that, if it were not for remarks such as the above, Russell would often sound like a "traditional Bodhisattva." As evidence, Ruland quotes Russell on his own life: "Love and knowledge, so far as they are possible, led upward toward the heavens. But always pity brought me back to earth. Echoes of cries of pain reverberate in my heart" (p. 107). As we have seen, what ties Bodhisattvas to this earth is their compassion for those still suffering. Indeed, Russell (1963) expressed some admiration for early Buddhism because, of the major religions, "it has the smallest element of persecution" (p. 203). Thus, one of the greatest objections humanists like Russell direct at religions is their lack of humanity.

Many humanist objections are, however, intellectual. Karl Marx—who, like Russell, was driven at least in part by compassion and outrage—saw religion as a ridiculous intellectual position. Were he alive today, he might agree wholeheartedly that we should teach about religion in the schools. A study of comparative religions, Marx thought, would show students how foolish their own beliefs were: "Bring your gods to a land where other gods prevail . . . and everybody will laugh at your subjective imagination" (quoted in Ruland, 1985, p. 110). Martin Gardner, the committed theist, agrees in part with Marx on this. He rejects biblical stories of miracles. Recounting several of Christianity's treasured miracle stories, Gardner (1983) says, "These are typical miracle tales of the sort no intelligent Christians would believe for a moment if they came upon them in the Koran" (p. 344). Marx and some other humanists see intellectual nonsense, and reject both God and religion. Gardner and like-minded theists see the same phenomena and find it possible to reject the nonsense and retain a strong faith in God. Some (though not Gardner) even remain in institutional religions.

For Marx and his followers, of course, Christianity was not just an intellectual error but a political one of monumental significance. Used as both a threat and an empty promise, Christianity kept the masses docile. "Religion," wrote Marx, "is the sign of the oppressed creature, the heart of a heartless world. . . . The abolition of religion as people's illusory happiness is the demand for their real happiness" (quoted in Ruland, 1985, p. 112). Marx wanted workers to see their actual condition and work to overthrow the powers responsible for it.

Freud expressed a different view of religion and of humanism. He saw religion as a sort of neurosis—a sign that humankind had not grown up. But, in contrast to Marx, he had no eschatological vision. Growing up was better than remaining an emotional child, but the achievement did not promise happiness. Freud belongs with the pessimists, and, indeed, he said that his pessimism was a conclusion reached after much observation, analysis, and reflection. The optimism of other thinkers, Freud claimed, was *a priori*—a premise undisturbed by honest observation of the human condition.

To those studying questions of belief and unbelief, the case of Freud and his dissident colleague, Jung, is fascinating. Agreeing on the historical record that shows humankind's universal interest in gods over all time, Freud saw a vast uncured neurosis; Jung saw the psychic reality of God.

Hans Kung also takes the intellectual objections of atheism and humanism seriously. Seeing and acknowledging many of the problems that have been raised throughout this book, Kung (1980) writes:

> But what if God really did not exist and never had existed? . . . We must ask ourselves very seriously: What would it mean for mankind if all signs of religion, from the graves of the Stone Age, the cave drawings of Altamira and the pyramids of Egypt, up to present-day grave tokens of death and eternal life, had really been set up for nothing? If all the wonderful churches and temples from Salamanca to Agra—the finest works of art ever produced by mankind—had really been built for a nothing? If all the great thinkers from the ancient Hindus and Greeks up to the moderns had really been thinking about a pure nothing? (p. 339)

Jean-Paul Sartre (1977), for one, would answer that these great works need not point to God, nor should they be construed as a mark of essential "man." Rather, they should be seen as the choices made by human beings who, in the name or service of whatever, involved themselves in great works. The existence of art, thought, and artifact proves only that some human being produced them and, therefore, that such works are possible for human beings.

It should be clear from this brief introductory discussion that the decision for belief or unbelief is not made entirely on intellectual grounds, although there are both believers and unbelievers who would claim that it is thus made. But there are different forms of humanism, and they too are characterized by differences in attitude as much as in belief. Students should know something about some of the prominent forms.

DETERMINISTIC HUMANISM

Whether a humanist can really be a determinist is a question raised by some thinkers. One can surely be an atheist and a determinist, but what can it mean to be a humanist determinist? As a determinist, these critics say, one cannot believe in progress, and as a (nonreligious) humanist, one cannot believe that the determined universe of events will all come out right eventually according to God's plan.

William James (1899) saw only two alternatives for determinists—pessimism or subjectivism. If every event is foreordained, if our beliefs about good and evil cannot influence our actual choices, what hope have we for a better world? Everything is as it must be. Regret, in such a world, is illogical. As James put it, "Calling a thing bad means, if it mean anything at all, that the thing ought not to be, that something else ought to be in its stead" (p. 161). There is no point in regretting something if, logically, there is not and never was any possibility that it could have been otherwise.

In his essay on determinism, James did not say much about religious determinism, but we may suppose from his few remarks that he would have placed it with subjectivism. A religious determinist would have to say, with Augustine and Leibniz, that the apparent horrors of this world all fit in some great plan that is overridingly good. Such thinkers escape pessimism by denying that evil is really, objectively evil.

> Even cruelty and treachery may be among the absolutely blessed fruits of time, and to quarrel with any of their details may be blasphemy. The only real blasphemy, in short, may be that pessimistic temper of soul which lets it give way to such things as regrets, remorse, and grief. (James, 1899, p. 163)

Nineteenth century literature is filled with the nonreligious form of subjectivism described by James. Accepting the scientific truth of determinism, writers construed feelings and attitudes as the whole point of human existence. In this romantic view, we cannot change things, but we can accept them nobly or cravenly; we can see and revel in beauty, or keep our eyes cast down on the dirt. From a religious perspective, the point of life is soul-making; from a humanistic perspective, it is knowledge and enlightenment.

It may be useful for students to learn something about the lives of real people who have leaned toward deterministic humanism. Clarence Darrow, the defender of John Scopes in the great evolution trial, is an interesting example. Throughout his adult life, Darrow took the position that it was a mistake to charge criminals with moral culpability because they really had no control over what they did (Tierney, 1979). They were *caused* to commit the deeds for which they were tried.

Darrow took this deterministic argument to its heights in defending Richard Loeb and Nathan Leopold, two wealthy Chicago teenagers, who murdered a boy they scarcely knew as a kind of experiment in planning and executing the perfect crime. This crime, which understandably outraged Chicago, was not committed by unfortunate victims of poverty and abuse. Darrow argued, first, that they were genetically impaired—that neither boy had the normal feelings of moral sensitivity or affection found in most people. Second, he argued that Leopold had been adversely influenced by the philosophy of Nietzsche taught at the University of Chicago. The university, Darrow claimed, was as guilty as Leopold! (This argument should logically have led Darrow to endorse censorship to eliminate such causes of crime, but the evidence suggests that he was strongly opposed to censorship. Even great lawyers lapse occasionally into illogicality!)

It is important for teenagers to hear this kind of argument. Hearing it paraphrased (without Darrow's dazzling rhetoric), they are likely to reject it. After all, lots of people read Nietzsche without becoming murderers. But what about contemporary pleas for criminals and rioters who are said to be caused to commit their crimes by poverty or racial oppression? What about Charles Manson, whose case we discussed earlier? Should he be less severely judged because he was influenced (mistakenly) by Eastern religion? Many of us do lean this way. James wanted students to understand that, if we excuse evildoers on the grounds that they could not have done otherwise, it makes little sense to call on the rest of us to make conditions better. Either things will get better or they won't. James leaves us with a reasonable pluralism: Conditions affect but do not determine human action; chance is real—a real phenomenon in the physical universe, and it includes free will; we make choices among genuine alternatives, and our regrets and moral judgments are not just empty attitudes.

We might decide that deep down Darrow must have believed something like this, too. How could he have exhorted juries and judges to do the right thing, how could he have worked so hard for social reform if he did not believe that he and his listeners had some control over what they chose to do? But it is not clear that Darrow *did* see the flaws in his deterministic reasoning. It is just as likely that he had a thoroughly romantic-subjectivist view, that he saw himself as a great actor on a stage peopled by fellow actors playing victims, judges, heroes, and villains. Certainly, he espoused fatalism all his life, and he did not escape pessimism.

In discussing whether evildoers should be treated gently because something in their past is really the cause of their behavior, teachers may have to suggest many examples to find out how carefully students have thought through their positions. Many may express sympathy for Manson, even more for the Los Angeles rioters, perhaps fewer for Leopold and Loeb. How many will express sympathy for members of the Nazi high command described by Alice Miller as products of faulty religious upbringing?

Students might be interested to hear that, despite the apparent philosophical difficulties, deterministic humanists have often been leaders in social reform movements. Indeed, arguments have been made that human responsibility makes sense *only* in a deterministic universe. "It is important to realize that determinism does not imply events occur *in spite of* our actions. Some events occur because *we* determine them" (Davies, 1983, p. 138). The alternative, Davies writes, is indeterminism. From this view, everything happens by chance, and how can we hold human beings responsible for chance occurrences? Others argue that neither total determinism nor complete chance governs the universe (Baudrillard, 1990). Lest students accept Davies's argument linking determinism to responsibility too easily, discussion should press the question of just how "we determine" events. That we are part of the causal chain seems obvious, but do our beliefs, choices, and decisions explain what we do, or must we look at prior physical causes? Put this question, students might not be so content with determinism. Darrow's determinism, in contrast to that of philosophers, seems not to have been carefully thought out, but it is a common view and one that many students may also hold: People are shaped by their environments and, at the same time, they have the capacity to change that environment.

There is another facet of Darrow's thought that is worth discussing here. He was a lifelong opponent of religion. In the Scopes trial, he savagely attacked the simplicity and backwardness of his opponent, William Jennings Bryan, pressing on him questions whose answers would make him appear either dishonest or hopelessly unsophisticated.

> If God is good, why does He permit pain? If the universe reveals a divine purpose, what is it? Is it immoral to learn a foreign language because, since the fall of the Tower of Babylon, God has intended that we speak different languages? How long is it since the Creation? Was Jonah really swallowed by a whale? (Tierney, 1979, p. 367)

Darrow's cruelty to Bryan contrasted sharply with the compassion that usually accompanied his humanism. But his antagonism to religion was steady. He worked diligently with leaders of the NAACP, almost all of whom shared his low opinion of religion. In Chapter 3, we discussed the important and salutary role of the black church in the lives of African Americans. In exploring Darrow's life and times, we have an opportunity to discuss the opposing view. Like Frederick Douglass before them, Walter White and James Weldon Johnson agreed with Darrow that religion was the enemy—not the savior—of black people. Darrow delivered his famous line to Johnson, "I am not interested in God and he is not interested in the colored people" (Tierney, 1979, p. 397).

Everywhere, as James (1899) noted, subjective determinism tends to aggravate the attitudes of those who espouse it. "Everywhere it fosters the fatalistic mood of mind. It makes those who are already too inert more passive still; it renders wholly reckless those whose energy is already in excess" (p. 171). James might well have been talking about characters like Darrow. Certainly Darrow displayed reckless—and highly effective—rhetoric in his defense of the killers, Loeb and Leopold, bringing tears to the eyes of almost everyone in the courtroom and, again, in his relentless attack on Bryan's fundamentalism. But rejection of determinism, in either its religious or humanistic forms, leaves us with a complicated and, at least from James's perspective, pluralistic universe—one with no unity from origin to eternity. James himself said that those loving unity would find his position unacceptable.

> A friend with such a mind once told me that the thought of my universe made him sick, like the sight of the horrible motion of a mass of maggots in their carrion bed. (p. 177)

To understand that reaction, students may have to learn a great deal more about the implications of a pluralistic universe. But let's turn now to another form of humanism, one that carries a title familiar to James but, otherwise, bears little resemblance to his views.

PRAGMATIC HUMANISM

When James spoke of a pragmatic view of religion, he had in mind not a scientific, naturalistic view of religion but an everyday notion of God as "absolute world-ruler"—as a personality who speaks to us and is heard by us. James's (1902/1958) view is pragmatic in this ordinary sense, in his emphasis on experience (as opposed to mere contemplation), and in his characteristic statement of pragmatic belief: "God is real since he produces real effects" (p. 389). In this sense, Jung was also pragmatic.

But James did not try to unify religion and science, nor did he try to redefine the common notion of God. He had great respect for thoughtful mystics and ascetics. Embracing the notion of a pluralistic universe and, perhaps, a God within time for whom the future is not entirely clear in every detail, he held to a God who has personality— a God move lovable than a cosmic force. He wrote:

> In whatever respects the divine personality may differ from ours or may resemble it, the two are consanguineous at least in this,—that both have purposes for which they care, and each can hear the other's call. (1899, p. 122)

His fellow pragmatist, John Dewey, took a very different stand. In Chapter 2, I mentioned Dewey's (1934) redefinition of God as the "active relation between ideal and actual" (p. 51) in individual and collective human life. Dewey's is a thoroughgoing scientific view. Theoretically, the presence of "God" in a person's life can be measured by his or her activity in the direction of an ideal. Dewey apparently believed that religious thought and language were too important to abandon, and so he attempted to give them new, scientific meaning and, hence, greater credibility.

Dewey (1934) sought a "common faith" that would not divide people into classes or sects, and he thought such a faith could be found in devotion to inquiry and commitment to the betterment of humankind. His secular humanism is, by his own admission, religious, but he did not want it to become *a* religion. In his characteristic approach, he rejected religion as a noun; he wanted to be rid of organizations devoted to anything supernatural, dogmatic, or doctrinal. But he wanted to retain the "religious," an adjectival label for experience that inspires us to surpass our present selves toward something better.

Believing that religion, like all of human thought, is a product of particular cultures, Dewey sought a concept of the religious that would be compatible with modern scientific society. Deeply influenced by Darwin, Dewey wanted "religious" to point to a way of life and a mode of experience that recognizes adaptation. To accommodate is legitimate if conditions demand accommodation, but it is better to manipulate conditions in our favor than to merely undergo them stoically. Thus Dewey (1934) invited an active sense of "religious," of committed action. Indeed, he insisted, "The essentially unreligious attitude is that which attributes human achievement and purpose to man in isolation from the world of physical nature and his fellows" (p. 25). Thus, connection was central to Dewey's idea of the religious, but it was connection on this earth that concerned him, not connection to an other-world deity. To be religious, for Dewey, was to be passionate in inquiry and humane commitment.

Dewey (1934) was also sensitive to the extremes of pessimism and optimism induced by religion (Christianity in particular). On the one hand, pessimism is aroused by the emphasis on "the corruption and impotency of natural means." But, writes Dewey, "This apparent pessimism has a way of suddenly changing into an exaggerated optimism" (p. 46). Whereas human beings and their means are evil and puny, God's are good and mighty, and so even horrendous acts and events can be justified in God's name. Human beings are made at once too helpless and too aggressive. Quiescence, not activity, marks the traditional religious attitude.

Emphasizing connection again, Dewey (1934) wrote against this quiescent attitude.

> A religious attitude, however, needs the sense of a connection of man, in the way of both dependence and support, with the enveloping world that the imagination feels is a universe. Use of the words "God" or "divine" to convey the union of actual with ideal may protect man from a sense of isolation and from consequent despair or defiance. (p. 53)

Dewey satisfied neither theists nor atheists, and he recognized and remarked on the precariousness of his own position. A God with no personality, a God reduced to a process, is, for theists, no God at all. And an atheist who can't bring himself to abandon God-talk is thought by more outspoken atheists to be weak-kneed and wishy-washy.

Gardner (1983), for one, was not impressed with Dewey's effort. Although he admired the honesty of atheists and agnostics like Russell, George Santayana, and H. G. Wells, he found Dewey totally lacking in a sense of the numinous.

> Nothing seems ever to have mystified Dewey. Never, so far as I can recall, did he see anything tragic or comic or absurd about the human condition. We are all organisms interacting with our environment, and that's that. (p. 335)

Gardner is a bit hard on Dewey, but others have also lost patience with atheists who are not honest enough to own up to their position. Nietzsche, for example, was outraged by both Ernst Haeckel and David Strauss. Both men, deeply influenced by Darwin and natural science, substituted the self-creating universe for the old, personal God. With the new faith in science came a buoyant optimism. Nietzsche found this a "shameless Philistine optimism." This religion of Haeckel and Strauss (and Gardner would add, of Dewey) was no religion at all: "At bottom, therefore, the religion is not a new belief, but, being of a piece with modern science, it has nothing to do with religion at all" (quoted in Kung, 1980, p. 350). Nietzsche could not abide this linguistic legerdemain, and heaped scorn on those he saw as timid atheists.

Many students are, however, attracted to views like Dewey's. They want to keep alive something of their childhood faith, and the notion of activating an ideal serves to maintain some connection to the God-concept. It also gives us a place as individual organisms in the societal organism that is striving toward perfection. This notion would bring a snort of contempt from Nietzsche, who felt that the redefinition of God in scientific terms could be traced more accurately to Hegel than to Darwin. By way of explanation for this wayward behavior, Nietzsche wrote, "He who has once sickened on Hegel . . . never completely recovers" (Kung, 1980, p. 350). This comment would, of course, apply to Dewey. It was the optimism of the scientific position as much as its fake religion that disgusted Nietzsche. He agreed with Schopenhauer that optimism was not merely absurd, "*but a vicious attitude of mind,* and one of scornful irony towards the indescribable sufferings of humanity" (Kung, 1980, p. 350).

Still, we can hear James's earlier diagnosis—that pessimism is essentially a religious disease, one engendered by religious disappointment. What Dewey and like-minded thinkers tried to do was to give humans a common faith in their own ability to control their lives and futures—to bring into being a new world scientifically and democratically guided. One question for students persuaded by Dewey's vision is: Should we call this vision "God"? Another is: Is scientific progress a convincing eschatology?

EXISTENTIAL HUMANISM

Existentialists, like pragmatists, differ in their approaches to religion. Some, like Kierkegaard, Marcel, and Buber, are deeply religious. Others are unbelievers. All put great emphasis on human responsibility and choice. Here we are primarily concerned with the humanism of existentialist unbelievers.

In contrast to determinists, existentialists like Jean-Paul Sartre posit the absolute freedom of human beings. There are those who criticize this position as tantamount to determinism, for—if human choice is totally unconditioned—in what sense is it genuine choice? Is complete caprice preferable to complete conditioning? Teachers who are interested in philosophical debate may want to pursue these questions in some depth, but the purpose of discussion with high school students is not to learn and recite the types of humanism, or to engage in analytic debate over technical philosophical issues (unless they want to). Rather, the purpose is to help students ask and explore questions that matter deeply in their own lives.

It may be important for some students to know that existentialist humanism insists that human beings are wholly responsible for what they make of themselves. In opposition to Darrow, who felt it was wrong to hold unfortunate people responsible for crimes they "had been driven to," Sartre wanted to hold each of us responsible not only for our own lives but for the condition of the whole society in which we participate. Human beings, said Sartre (1977), are not thrown into the world with an essential nature; neither are they unwillingly molded by their encounters in the world. Existence, reflective living, precedes essence. This means that

> Man exists, turns up, appears on the scene, and, only afterwards, defines himself. If man, as the existentialist conceives him, is indefinable, it is because at first he is nothing. Only afterward will he be something,

and he himself will have made what he will be. Thus there is no human nature, since there is no God to conceive it. (p. 36)

Sartre (1977), of course, recognized human facticity. He agreed that we are affected by heredity, by the limitations of our animal organism, by the privileges we receive or are denied. But our essential selves are made by us. "Man is at the start a plan which is aware of itself, rather than a patch of moss, a piece of garbage, or a cauliflower" (p. 36). Sartre said that we are responsible for both the plan and its enactment.

Forms of humanism that elevate humans *as a type* annoyed Sartre. He had little patience for the scientific humanism of the pragmatists, although he agreed with them in their emphasis on action and consequences. What he deplored was the substitution of scientific or ideological progress for religious salvation. He also thought that the humanists who claimed that the moral universe remained intact without God were terribly mistaken. They traded faith in one absolute for faith in another just as shaky. They did not see the great abyss opened by the loss of God.

The existentialist, on the contrary, thinks it very distressing that God does not exist, because all possibility for finding values in a heaven of ideas disappears along with Him; there can no longer be an *a priori* Good, since there is no infinite and perfect consciousness to think it. (Sartre, 1977, pp. 40–41)

Recognition of God's nonexistence leaves us forlorn. This forlornness is part of our common condition, and Sartre felt that those who deny it are dishonest. Along with forlornness goes anguish. As we understand the magnitude of our freedom and responsibility, we cannot help but suffer anguish. We must choose ourselves and, as we do so, we help to define all of humankind. Our lives—each of them—show what a person can be. Those who excuse themselves to themselves (as Darrow excused criminals) are cowards; those who deny to the world the freedom they inwardly know they possess are stinkers (Sartre, 1977, p. 58). Heroes and cowards are not born heroic or cowardly; they make themselves what they are. Contrasting existentialism with Ayn Rand's "objectivism," Hazel Barnes (1978) notes the dogmatic and rigid character of the latter.

The rules are laid down and written out. Best of all, one need never ask whether the game is really worth playing or what constitutes good

sportsmanship. The existentialist, on the other hand, confronts his freedom in anguish. What he sees is not a two-fold choice as definite as the
old one which Christianity offered. He realizes that all is open. His
freedom is not just the choice between thinking and not thinking, between seeing what is right or refusing to see it. He knows that being
free means creating standards of right and wrong. It means that there is
no one right pattern for man, but many possible patterns to be discov-
ered and invented. God Almighty has not been deposed merely in order
that Mother Nature—or Daddy Warbucks—might sit there, passing out
blueprints. (p. 133)

Why would an existentialist humanist be moral? This is a question we will discuss more fully in Chapter 7, but here we need to say
at least that Sartre did not believe that loss of God and utter freedom
meant chaos or caprice. A moral life is planned, composed, enacted
like a work of art. Sartre (1977) used painting as an analogy. Just as
we do not say that a successful artist should have painted some other
picture, so we cannot "decide *a priori* what there is to be done"
(pp. 55–56) in moral life. Each person must choose, but he or she is
responsible for that choice and must honestly face its consequences
as they are reflected in the eyes of those affected by them.

Existentialist and deterministic views may serve as mutual cor-
rectives. A good dose of existentialism may force deeper thought on
those who lean toward a liberal, determinist view. The heroes and
antiheroes of existentialist literature—of Camus, Dostoevsky, Kafka,
and Sartre—may bring students to a fuller understanding of human
responsibility. On the other side, the despair and nausea of existentialism may be countered by accounts of hard-working, compassionate determinists like Darrow and B. F. Skinner who insisted that
those who could *should* change societal conditions so that people
would be shaped for better lives. Skinner's (1962) *Walden Two* illustrates the theoretical possibilities for a better life in a deterministic
universe. Similarly, Orwell's (1949) *Nineteen Eighty-Four* illustrates
the possibilities of complete evil in a world where people are condi-
tioned ruthlessly.

THE GROWTH OF HUMANISM

Many people today take the freedom to be unbelievers for
granted but, actually, unbelief has been generally accessible for only
a little over one hundred years (J. Turner, 1985). Even today, a thor-

oughly humanist position—a confessed unbelief in God—would probably prevent a person from holding a prominent political post in this country. Although there have always been unbelievers, people in the past were not able to choose unbelief as they might Presbyterianism or Catholicism.

Nineteenth century thinkers who dared to challenge traditional forms of belief often paid dearly for their convictions. I mentioned earlier the contempt Nietzsche heaped on David Friedrich Strauss for his failure to accept the logical conclusions of his own study and embrace an honest position of unbelief. But Strauss (1846), in his *Life of Jesus*, did not intend to destroy either Christianity or belief in God. He wanted, rather, to demystify both. The reaction was condemnation by traditional Christians and contempt from atheists like Nietzsche. Strauss lost his academic job and, indeed, his whole academic career. So much for academic freedom in Germany in the mid-nineteenth century!

Strauss suggested an idea, however, that has remained at the heart of some forms of humanism. Labeling the dogma of Jesus as God-man a mythology, he substituted humanity as god-men. According to Strauss, all of humanity, not just rare incarnations, are gods and responsible for their own destinies. As god-men, humans are perfectible, manifesting the infinite in the finite. As we have seen, this is a form of humanism rejected by Sartre on the grounds that it posits an *a priori* human nature. It was also rejected by Russell, who worried about putting such emphasis on humankind in a universe where so many other phenomena seemed even more important—or, at least, more interesting.

From the mid-nineteenth century, interest in humanism grew as doubts about Christianity increased. Many of the doubts were triggered by the cruelty in religious doctrine. In an age of growing humanitarianism, belief in a God who visited evil into the third and fourth generations and condemned a multitude of souls to eternal hell seemed immoral. Thus, an enlightened perspective on morality and an awakened intolerance for unnecessary pain actually worked against belief. Historical studies like those of Strauss contributed to the doubts. How, after all, could the Absolute be found in history? And if the historical truth of events such as the Resurrection were discarded, what remained of Christianity? (J. Turner, 1985). Studies in geology and Darwin's exposition of evolution added further doubts.

Interestingly, comparative religion was also a powerful force in shaking the faith of many Christian thinkers, and this tends to support Marx's contention that one's own beliefs often look silly in light of another's religion.

> President Andrew Dickson White of Cornell recalled that his belief in Christ's miracles, on which Christian truth seemed to depend, collapsed in the 1850s when he learned that Islam claimed the same sort of evidence for its doctrines. And Charles Eliot Norton, son of the "Unitarian Pope" Andrews Norton, found himself almost chuckling at the irony when a Westminster Abbey congregation prayed for the conversion of the heathen. (J. Turner, 1985, p. 155)

In previous chapters, we have seen that many of the rituals and dogmas of contemporary Christianity have antecedents in earlier "pagan" religions, and Judaism frankly admits to developing many of its doctrines by inverting previously held ideas. But, although such disclosures are enough to drive some mature thinkers into unbelief, many others find a larger sense of the sacred in the universal practices of religion. Of these latter, some become deists or noninstitutional theists, but a surprising number retain a demythologized Christianity or an unorthodox Judaism.

Present-day loss of faith in the humanism of Marx and Freud and even Strauss has, perhaps, contributed to the revival religion seems to be experiencing (Stark & Bainbridge, 1985). All over the world, fundamentalism—apparently in all the major religions—is enjoying new power. This is as worrisome to humanists as the earlier humanist challenges were to Christianity. For educators this trend is much more worrisome, for humanism in most of its forms urges critical examination of the issues and conscious responsibility for positions taken, but fundamentalism rejects such critical analysis as sinful. Alan Peshkin (1986) describes the views of one fundamentalist school head.

> McGraw [the school head] presents the "five basic tenets of humanism" as: (1) atheism; (2) immorality; (3) evolution; (4) the belief that man can do anything he wants to do; and (5) ecumenism. (p. 77)

The unfairness of this evaluation of humanism is obvious; the ignorance it reveals is shocking. Although education for intelligent belief or unbelief involves compassionate and appreciative examination of all religious views, it may be impossible to discuss fundamentalism without threatening fundamentalist tenets. If it is a sin to subject one's beliefs to critical analysis, how can schools insist on such analysis? This is a problem I will discuss in greater depth in Chapter 8. Here we can only conclude that humanism—religious or nonreligious—seems more compatible with both education and democracy than does fundamentalism or related religious attitudes.

Harold Bloom (1992) castigates the uncritical, highly personal, fundamentalist attitude—a view he calls "the American religion."

> Urging the need for community upon American religionists is a vain enterprise; the experiential encounter with Jesus or God is too overwhelming for memories of community to abide, and the believer returns from the abyss of ecstasy with the self enhanced and otherness devalued. . . . How are we to understand, and judge, an American spirituality that, to be authentic, seems always fated to make the believer, ultimately, a worse citizen, despite all the blatherings of our ideology? (p. 27)

Bloom points here to the highly individualistic nature of American religion—its insistence that every true Christian must have a direct encounter with Jesus and believe that "Jesus loves me." In his critical analysis, Bloom does not include mainstream branches of Christianity except to note that their spiritual vigor (as opposed to their social energy) often resembles that of fundamentalism. In this sense, "the American religion" tends to be dogmatic, individualistic, and self-righteous, and its character affects national politics. Bloom (1992) comments:

> President George Bush, whatever other eminence awaits him, is already bound to be memorable as the American leader most deeply attached to linked emblems of our national religion: the flag and the fetus, our Cross and our Divine Child. The flag and the fetus together symbolize the American Religion, the partly concealed but scarcely repressed national faith. (p. 45)

Bloom needs to give far more support than he has for such a sweeping indictment, but the cumulative effects of his analysis of particular sects—even if those effects are not so clearly pronounced at the national level—are frightening enough. If educators believe in the cultivation of critical intelligence, they had better insist on their right to work at it and get busy challenging the nonsense that seems to be growing everywhere.

CHAPTER 7

Religious and Secular Ethics

People often suppose that moral life depends on God and that children especially need religious training to be good persons. Indeed, some of the world's great ethical systems have been anchored in belief, and the loss of God—as we heard Sartre say—lays a heavy responsibility on human agents to decide on the moral values to which they will commit themselves. In stark contrast to the common notion that belief is necessary for moral life, many nineteenth century thinkers began to evaluate belief itself as immoral (J. Turner, 1985). The cruelty of the God portrayed in large parts of the Bible, the intellectual foolishness of much religious dogma, the proliferation of religions and sects all claiming unique access to Truth, the bloodshed and torture resulting from religious fervor—all of these led some people to discard belief, and even campaign vigorously against it.

Until the last two centuries of the Christian era, religion had almost a monopoly on moral teaching. It taught people how they should relate to God, to individuals with whom they might interact, to the community of believers, and to the world at large. Then reason began to replace faith, and nonreligious humanism became an option. People interested in moral life could continue to follow the dictates of their religion, or they could revive an Aristotelian-communitarian ethic (MacIntyre, 1984), or they could deny that anything had changed with the loss of belief in God, or they could start from scratch as advised by Nietzsche and Sartre. This chapter looks at both religious and secular ethics as they are influenced by belief or unbelief. We start with an aspect of moral life central to religious ethics and rarely touched by secular ethics—personal morality. Then we will look at the moral agent in direct interaction, at moral life in a well-defined community, and finally at ethics and social responsibility.

PERSONAL MORALITY

Religious moral theory has always put tremendous emphasis on the relation of each human being to God. To be right with God is the first and greatest obligation of believers. In some religions and sects, believers can earn merit by behaving compassionately and fairly toward other human beings (or all living things); in others, no merit can possibly be earned, and believers are justified only by faith and grace. Even in the latter, good works have a place; although they cannot earn merit, they are often taken as a sign that the doer is one of the elect. Practice is never irrelevant, and it is certainly a factor to be considered by anyone striving for intelligent belief or unbelief.

Hans Kung (1980) says that, although practice cannot be the only criterion of the truth of belief in God, belief is nevertheless "proved in practice."

> Believers in God who live in a truly human way are an argument for that belief. But the reverse is also true: Believers in God who do not live in a truly human way are an argument against that belief. (p. 326)

How should we describe this truly human way of life that reflects positively on belief in God?

This is a question that divides religious communities even today. Fundamentalist groups tend to emphasize personal morality and the individual's relation to God. Others—religious humanists in particular—put far greater emphasis on the social actions of believers. In Christianity, some mainline churches have suffered schisms over just these issues.

Many Protestant groups have insisted on the separation of the social and the sacred. The main job of the church, in this view, is to tell the gospel and to put people in touch with saving grace through belief. If these people, once saved, want to engage in positive social action, that is up to them, but the church's job is salvation—not social or political action. Writing of Martin Luther's position on this question, Alasdair MacIntyre (1966) says:

> We could not be further away from Aristotle; he is, said Luther, "that buffoon who has misled the church." The true transformation of the individual is entirely internal; to be before God in fear and trembling as a justified sinner is what matters. . . . Luther's demand that we attend only to faith and not to works is accompanied by prohibitions uttered against certain types of work. He condemned peasant insurrec-

tion and advocated the massacre by their princes of peasant rebels against lawful authority. (p. 122)

Religions that concentrate on the relation of person to God and on personal salvation put correspondingly great emphasis on the concept of sin. Sin is a transgression against God and God's rules, and the remedy is, variously, direct confession or confession mediated by the church and repentance. Secular ethicists often find this emphasis repugnant because moral agents are distracted from the wrongs and harms they inflict on other human beings and directed to their own salvation. For example, religious morality usually instructs us not to kill. "Thou shalt not kill," is one of God's commandments. But, of course, God apparently makes exceptions, and believers are often directed to kill in the name of some great cause or, even, in the actual name of God. For secular ethicists, this is reason enough to discard belief. In fairness, however, they must admit that secular ethicists, too, can construct justifications for acting against their own basic principles.

Part of the humanistic objection to the various doctrines on sin can be located in their reliance on and promotion of authority. To claim that humankind is born in a condition of original sin is to establish the need for salvation. This need in turn directs sinners either to submit to the authority of the church or to spend an almost obsessive amount of time in communication with God. In the former case, rational reflection is likely to be blocked; in the latter, normal pursuit of worldly pleasure and even worldly duties is likely to be reduced. The great feminist, Elizabeth Cady Stanton, spoke of her eventual rejection of Christian orthodoxy as a form of liberation.

> In the darkness and gloom of a false theology, I was slowly sawing off the chains of my spiritual bondage, when, for the first time, I met [William Lloyd] Garrison in London. A few bold strokes from the hammer of his truth, and I was free! Only those who have lived all their lives under the dark clouds of vague, undefined fears can appreciate the joy of a doubting soul suddenly born into the kingdom of reason and free thought. Is the bondage of the priest-ridden less galling than that of the slave, because we do not see the chains, the indelible scars, the festering wounds, the deep degradation of all the powers of the Godlike mind? (J. Turner, 1985, p. 210)

Testimonies of this sort proliferated in the nineteenth century. On the other hand, so did testimonies from those newly saved, and even today we hear both fictional and biographical accounts of those whose lives have been affected for the better by their conversion to religious belief. For example, the twelve-step programs that seem to be springing up everywhere usually involve belief in a higher power and, often, in an orthodox saving grace.

Besides its support for institutional authority, the doctrine of original sin promoted attention to the soul over the body. It directed thought toward the corruption of the flesh and toward personal morality. No mainstream secular ethic puts such emphasis on individual sexual behavior as does religious morality. Secular ethics are concerned with the harm and hurt we may cause others by our sexual behavior but not with the "sin" we commit by the very nature of our acts. No secular ethic condemns bodily pleasure in itself; only if its pursuit indicates neglect of clear moral duties is it suspect. As we have already seen, the doctrine also did enormous harm to women, whose subordination was justified by the church's interpretation of the Fall. All told, the harm has been considerable.

Although it is certainly true that religious belief keeps many young people from committing deeds that are unhealthy, unlawful, or harmful to others, often it also keeps them from reflecting deeply on the nature of the deity in whom they believe. It is in this area that the school has a special obligation. Without endorsing belief or unbelief, the school should be sure that students hear the eloquent objections of great thinkers. Stanton thought it ridiculous to suppose that the universe was guided by a "tender loving fatherly intelligence"; John Stuart Mill refused to call him "good" unless God could measure up on at least the standards human beings apply to one another. James Turner (1985) writes further:

> Declarations of unbelief often sounded more like acts of moral will than intellectual judgments. [Robert] Ingersoll said that "I cannot worship a being" whose "cruelty is shoreless." Darwin was so appalled by the harshness of natural selection that he could no longer bring himself to believe in God: better that this horror should have sprung from blind chance. Or listen to Henry Adams, reacting to his sister's death: "The idea that any personal deity could find pleasure or profit in torturing a poor woman, by accident, with a fiendish cruelty known to man only in perverted and insane temperaments, could not be held for a moment. For pure blasphemy, it made pure atheism a comfort." (p. 207)

This particular dilemma is one with which all intelligent believers and unbelievers must deal. If God is a personal God—one who cares what we do to and with our bodies, who watches our every step— why is there so much suffering? And why, if *we* are commanded to love one another and to relieve suffering, does God not heed his own commandment? As Turner (1985) points out, the humanitarianism that arose within Christianity turned around to criticize the Christian God (p. 207).

Well-educated nineteenth century unbelievers (almost all of whom started out as believers) predicted the demise of religion—particularly in its personal form. Yet today, according to survey after survey, most Americans believe in a personal God, and many Christians profess the belief that "Jesus loves me" (Bloom, 1992). Indeed, all over the world there seems to be an increase in fundamentalist membership and a concomitant increase in the belief that God wants each individual to show his or her absolute faith in a personal, God-human relationship.

In Judaism, too, there seems to be an increased interest in forms of religion that require personal performance—the keeping of rules and practice of rituals. Like Christianity, Judaism has had its internal critics. Just as advocates of liberation theology have criticized the Catholic Church for its emphasis on individual soul-saving when whole societies desperately need reform, so Jewish thinkers like Martin Buber have criticized Judaism for its concentration on rules and rituals. Buber insisted that God is encountered through human beings.

Nontheistic religions also stress personal morality. Both Hinduism and Buddhism trace suffering to ignorance. Hence the religious quest in each is for knowledge of reality and self. In Hinduism, the true self is immortal. Life extends forever in both directions. Rodney Taylor (1989) quotes Krishna talking to the warrior Arjuna, who feels that he should not fight a battle in which relatives appear on the other side.

> "You grieve for those who should not be mourned. . . . The learned do not grieve for the dead or for the living. Never, indeed, was there a time when I was not, nor when you were not, nor these lords of men. Never, too, will there be a time, hereafter, when we shall not be." (p. 17)

One can see how a poorly educated person attracted to Eastern religion might misinterpret these words and suppose that killing is unimportant. Indeed, we saw in Chapter 3 that Charles Manson had apparently been influenced in just such a way.

Although the aim of religious knowledge in Hinduism is to overcome the false sense of individuality and realize the true self as an integral part of the universe, the quest itself is still personal. Morality is centered on *karma*. One must do right by others to avoid earned suffering in the next life and to pay off debts accrued in past lives. Like many forms of Christianity, Hinduism's morality includes a healthy dose of self-interest. Further, it may be criticized for its callous belief that *karma* justifies the caste system—that is, that people born into the lower castes earned their low status in a previous life. This belief is similar to one in the Calvinist tradition that marks prosperity and good fortune as signs of the elect, poverty and ill fortune as signs of the damned. Neither attitude passes the test of humanitarianism as secular humanists pose it.

Buddhism traces suffering not so much to a faulty view of reality as to craving and desire. The remedy is still knowledge, for if we realize that our pain is the common lot of all those who are attached to things in this world, we can try to overcome our attachments. The emphasis is, again, on personal behavior: Right Views, Right Resolve, Right Speech, Right Conduct, Right Livelihood, Right Effort, Right Mindfulness, and Right Concentration (the Noble Eightfold Path). There is something quite Kantian in Buddhism. One acts through and toward the fullest knowledge; one does not act out of inclination.

Buddhism, too, has been affected by the demand that religion pay more attention to humanitarian interests. The Bodhisattva figure (whom we met in the earlier discussion of salvation) is one of great compassion. The Bodhisattva has attained the perfect knowledge required for Nirvana but refuses to enter it until all those suffering can also do so. But, because the remedy for suffering is knowledge, the Bodhisattva is primarily teacher, not the direct reliever of pain.

In Western religions, adherents are instructed to accept suffering and find meaning in it. Faith is the remedy, not knowledge. The nineteenth century brought a great challenge to traditional Christianity. Many thinkers no longer accepted the notion that pain and suffering were part of God's great plan for us. Rather, as Oliver Wendell Holmes, Jr., said:

> We have learned the doctrine that evil means pain, and the revolt against pain in all its forms has grown more and more marked. From societies for the prevention of cruelty to animals up to socialism, we express in numberless ways the notion that suffering is wrong which can be and ought to be prevented, and a whole literature of sympathy has sprung into being. (quoted in J. Turner, 1985, p. 206)

RELATIONS TO INDIVIDUAL OTHERS

All religious ethics are concerned with how we should meet and treat other human beings. Nineteenth century humanism grew in part out of a sense that the God of Christianity and Judaism was not as ethically good as humans themselves wanted to be. Much of this discontent arose from a critical examination of religious literature. If we choose judiciously, however, we can find strong support for the proposition that religious ethics enjoin us to treat others with fairness and compassion. But do religious ethics give us anything in this area that secular ethics do not?

In trying to answer this question, we can look at two possibilities. Religious ethics may give us more powerful justification or more powerful motivation. I think it will be clear that we cannot get much out of the first possibility, but the second is more promising.

Religious ethics are often justified as the commandments of God. If one asks why the commandments of God should be obeyed, two answers are forthcoming. One says, roughly, because God is God and commands obedience; the second says, because God is good. This second answer lands us back in the difficulty of describing "good," and, as many humanists have pointed out, it may be difficult to show that God *is* good by any of our definitions. Thus the first response is the only uniquely religious justification for ethics. God defines what is good; our task is not to second-guess God but to obey. Now, of course, a new question arises: How do we know that any particular set of commandments really do represent God's commandments? Because religions and sects within religions differ dramatically in their answers to this, there is no universally compelling response. Why would God choose to speak Truth through a particular doctrine or a particular people—Jews, Christians, or Muslims?

Although most philosophers and many theologians would agree that religious ethics cannot provide unique justification for their pronouncements, the supposition that they do have such justification is widespread in the general populace. Take one current example. Why should women not be allowed the choice to have abortions? Both secular and religious arguments against abortion usually label it murder. The secular argument rests on the personhood or potential personhood of the fetus. The religious argument presses further and finds abortion (and sometimes even birth control) contrary to God's commandments. This claim provides no justification for those who either do not believe in God or who believe that God has given different commandments. But the motivational power of claiming God's will is still enormous for believers.

Both believers and unbelievers who feel that abortion is murder are determined to push for laws that will protect its victims. In the battle against slavery more than one hundred years ago, believers and unbelievers joined to condemn that practice. But believers were in the forefront. Their claim to be serving God's will was enormously powerful and attracted many followers. Similarly, those who fight abortion in God's name have, perhaps, greater persuasive power than those who use secular arguments. The latter are committed to the cause but often are also committed to rational argumentation and, therefore, have difficulty in establishing an absolute claim.

Debate on abortion may occur without discussion of religion or religious ethics. Thomas Lickona (1991), for example, has suggested guidelines for the classroom discussion of controversial issues, including abortion. But to omit the religious arguments is to ignore a long history of moral teaching and, some would say, of attempts by religious institutions to control the bodies of women. If such debate is to take place, students need considerably more information than Lickona provides in two short opposing essays. Above all, they need to understand the passion with which advocates and opponents approach the question and the difference it makes when one group claims that God is on its side. Religious ethics provide motivation. Even their claim to justification is a powerful motivation.

Some secular ethicists have tried to establish naturalistic ethics. The scheme of justification in such ethics is consequentialist but it need not be utilitarian. A naturalistic ethic tries to show that the results of behaving in a certain pattern are objectively better than results obtained by other patterns of behavior. Naturalistic ethics do not argue that each person must try out every possible behavior—such as killing and stealing—to see whether its consequences are favorable. The desirability of many acts was decided long ago, but the ultimate test was, and still is in times of indecision, whether the consequences are acceptable for all those involved or, if not acceptable to some, whether we have done the best we can. Naturalists, like existentialists, also put great emphasis on responsibility. According to Dewey, moral persons must be willing to accept responsibility for the acts they choose and the consequences thus engendered. They must say, "I knew X might occur if I did A, and I stand responsible for X."

A good Deweyan could not excuse an act (as a good Catholic might) by invoking the doctrine of double effect. According to this doctrine, if by doing *A* I intend to produce effect *Y*, and it is reasonable to suppose that *A* will effect *Y* and *Y* is morally permissible, then even if I know that *X* will likely also be a result—and *X* is morally undesirable—I may be justified in doing *A*. The doctrine of double effect has been used to excuse the killing of civilians by airmen who intended only the destruction of military targets—even though the likelihood of civilian casualties was known. It has also been used to justify allowing a mother to die rather than killing a preborn infant in a difficult birth. In this case, it is argued that not performing an abortion is intended to preserve the life of the child; the mother's death is not intended and, thus, the act is morally right although humanly regrettable. I am not arguing that a Deweyan cannot find any justification for doing *A*, only that he or she cannot use an argument like that of double effect—one that looks only at intentions and not at predictable consequences.

As students discuss arguments for and against various acts, they will find that religious and secular ethics do not differ much on what they assess as right and wrong (Hauerwas, 1983). Indeed, both try to conform to certain basic moral intuitions, although both usually reject intuition as an ultimate ground for moral decisions. For example, most religious and secular ethics find infanticide wrong, but they may give different reasons for their evaluations. In the cases considered above—of civilian casualties and abstaining from abortion—we could find secular ethics that would accept the argument of double effect. Thus there is nothing in the content of religious ethics—where they address themselves to the moral agent's conduct with respect to others—that separate them distinctly from secular ethics. As we saw in the first section, religious ethics do often differ in their pronouncements on personal morality (what the agent does with his or her own body and how the agent relates to higher powers), but even here the distinction is not absolute or universal, and where the distinction holds—on duties to God, for example—the category is not always labeled "moral."

Discussions of this sort need not be confined to formal classes on ethics. They may arise any time questions of the sort, Why should we do *A*? or Why may we do *B*? arise, and teachers should be prepared to help students engage in them.

In the discussion of controversial moral issues it is the job of teachers to be pedagogically neutral (Vandenberg, 1983); that is, teachers have an obligation to present all significant sides of an issue in their full passion and best reasoning. This is not to say that teachers should not disclose their own beliefs and commitments (although sometimes they should not), but that they should always help students to see why an issue *is* controversial. If it were settled, if the teacher's belief were necessarily right, there would be no controversy. Clearly, it can be very hard for teachers with strong religious commitments to maintain pedagogical neutrality, but they must be helped to understand that pedagogical neutrality is not the same as ethical neutrality. I may be completely convinced that abortion is usually morally acceptable and often morally obligatory and yet encourage a dialogue that brings forth the strong points in opposing positions and exposes the weaknesses in my own. In doing so, I make a special moral affirmation as a teacher: Students must be allowed, even encouraged, to ask how, why, and on what grounds (Scheffler, 1960).

If we agree that teachers have a moral obligation to pedagogical neutrality when controversial moral issues arise, we may still disagree on whether teachers should encourage or even allow such issues to arise. If the topic is not strictly part of the curriculum, should a teacher allow its discussion? This is itself a controversial issue that should be explored thoroughly in teacher education classes. Now, have I prejudiced the case by saying that *this* question *should be* explored? Not so long as the answer to the classroom question is still a possible "no" or "sometimes but not always." I could argue, more strongly perhaps, that it would be morally reprehensible not to discuss the question since the issue it addresses will inevitably arise in classrooms and teachers must be prepared to respond to it.

In summary, religious and secular ethics do not differ greatly on matters concerning how moral agents should meet and treat the abstract other. The secular optimists are right, in one sense, that we need not fear the loss of morality with the loss of God. In another sense, of course, they are wrong, because the ultimate justification traditionally used is gone, and, theoretically, everything is up for re-examination. Many of our most vexing moral problems can be addressed with the same effect through either religious or secular ethics, but it is vital to include religious approaches in our pedagogy. Students need to understand not only the content of an argument but the force of the beliefs behind it.

MORAL LIFE IN THE COMMUNITY

In Chapter 3, we saw that people are often drawn to religion by its promise of community. People want to belong to institutions and groups deemed worthy. Even though religious and secular ethics say roughly the same things about how moral agents should treat others, they differ practically along lines of affiliation. Religious ethics have a great deal more to say about the behavior of individuals with respect to their own souls, and they more often differentiate between people inside and outside the norm group. This can be both a strength and a weakness in religious ethics.

Members of most religious groups can expect help and support from their institutions in time of need. Religious groups pride themselves on taking care of their own. But religions can also whip up hatred of outsiders and promulgate pseudo-justifications for atrocious behavior. In the United States, our cruel, dishonest, and cavalier treatment of Native Americans was facilitated by the belief that we were dealing with "heathen savages." Similarly, as we saw in Chapter 3, many of the most horrible deeds in history have been instigated or backed by religious rationales.

Today, with increased emphasis on communitarian ethics, it is especially important to look at both the strengths and weaknesses of this approach to ethics. In general, communitarians believe that ethical thought arises in community life and that people behave morally because they have internalized the expectations of the community. Descriptively, communitarians seem right; most of us do use community expectations as a guide to moral behavior. But whether this behavior is good or bad depends on the status of the community's norms. Are *they* good or bad? If I am a member of a group that has spent centuries examining and re-examining its own moral life, reflecting critically on its own traditions, I may well be justified in following its dictates. However, if I am a member of some dogmatic cult or of a street gang, I may behave in ways that the larger society will regard as immoral. Thus, although the rules of a group can be a powerful motivator, they cannot themselves justify the ethical behavior they prescribe. Here religious ethics, a form of communitarian ethics, has a tremendous advantage over secular ethics: It appears to have the ultimate justification—God. As we saw earlier, however, this advantage is only apparent, because the question of what is good still has to be answered.

Philosophers care deeply about the problem of justification. They are always looking for a firmer grounding for ethical decisions. In moral education, debate continues over what constitutes the highest form of moral reasoning and, indeed, over whether reasoning should be regarded as the most important feature of ethical life. Followers of Lawrence Kohlberg (1981), for example, put great emphasis on knowledge and reasoning—more or less depending on the Platonic notion that to know the good is to do the good. Many others have grave doubts about depending so heavily on reasoning—pointing to the atrocious behavior of many people who are clearly able to reason at a high level. Further, there are admirable examples of people who have acted with moral heroism because they believed their community expected that kind of behavior from them. For example, Oliner and Oliner (1988) found that many non-Jewish rescuers of Jews during the holocaust acted compassionately—at great risk to themselves—because they had been raised in communities that expected compassion from their members. Thus, although tradition cannot justify itself at the theoretical level, individuals in a community can reliably anchor their behavior in tradition if that tradition is an ethically admirable one.

The fear of those opposed to communitarian ethics (and of many thoughtful proponents as well) is that people who justify their behavior in terms of group norms or traditions may be incapable of critiquing those traditions or, worse, may fall prey to immoral groups with strong authoritarian messages and group bonds. Most communitarian ethicists recognize these dangers and recommend ways of avoiding or minimizing them.

Both Aristotle and Confucius described forms of communitarian ethics. Both put great emphasis on the role of moral exemplars—people in the community thought to embody the highest virtues. Moral education in Confucianism consists of inculcating community values, developing virtues, and in general encouraging the development of character. Much attention is given in Confucianism to the proper enactment of various roles and to the rules that should govern various relationships. As a moral agent, one does not invoke an abstract principle of social justice to justify one's behavior; more often, the agent refers to a particular set of rules that govern one's behavior in relation to this particular person. Our obligations to parents, children, authorities, strangers, and friends differ and must be described in detail.

Confucianism has been criticized for its stress on specific relationships. It is not characterized by the impartiality that some modern thinkers insist should mark ethical thought and behavior. Confucians are not opposed to universal love and compassion, but they teach that moral relations must begin in the family and that people learn to care and to behave morally in ever-widening circles as they perfect their ways of relating in more intimate circles. Even at higher levels of perfection, however, the morally wisest people recognize that the obligation to, say, parents is different from that to strangers.

Many feminist ethicists today look favorably on the Confucian emphasis on *jen*, which might be translated as "person-to-person-ness" (Taylor, 1989, p. 24). In several forms of feminist ethics, we find a similar emphasis on the direct relation of person to person—in caring (Noddings, 1984), in communicative ethics (Benhabib, 1987), in maternal thinking (Ruddick, 1980, 1989). But, in all feminist ethics, there is an objection to hierarchy, and systems of ethics like that of Confucius or Aristotle are sharply criticized for identifying members of communities by their particular functions. In an ethic of care, for example, we do not justify treating people differently because they occupy different positions in the community but because they have different needs and because our capacities to meet those needs differ with our personal resources and with the expectations of those with whom we are in relation. Both the traditional ethics (Aristotelian and Confucian) and contemporary feminist ethics are criticized, however, for their stress on particular rather than universal (abstract) relations. In turn, both ethics look upon this stress as a great strength and find the emphasis on universality faulty both epistemologically and morally.

Confucian ethics, in its religious form, depends on the capacity of human beings for compassion. Like all religious ethics, then, it ultimately depends on God. In this case, God does not directly bestow laws on human conduct, but instead instills in every human being the capacity to feel the pain and joy of others. In Confucian moral education, this capacity is to be cultivated. Contemporary care theorists, too, emphasize the fundamental ability to care but trace it to being cared for effectively rather than to an initial gift from God. In both views, parents and teachers bear great responsibility for nurturing the capacity to care.

Both secular and religious forms of communitarian ethics have obvious strengths. They are convincing in describing the way people acquire and enact moral beliefs, and their attempts at justification are at least as effective as individualistic ethics. If God is not invoked as ultimate justification, communitarians must depend on a human connection that seems to be universally valued and on continual reflection on how this value motivates human behavior. At their best, communitarian ethics do not just encapsulate and enforce community values, but, rather, call into question, point out shortcomings, demand accounting, and point their people continually upward.

But there is a downside to communitarian ethics, and students should be made acutely aware of it. Even if they have never heard the word *communitarian*, chances are that their own ethical perspectives are somewhat communitarian. They emulate those they find admirable, and they are very much affected by peer pressure. School spirit, group loyalty, national patriotism, and religious denominationalism are all compatible with an unreflective communitarianism. All of these are signs of exclusionary thinking—a we–they, us–them attitude.

Religious ethics of all sorts have promoted, at the same time, both universal love and exclusionary thinking. On one level, believers are exhorted to love all God's creatures; on another, they are often encouraged to love believers more than unbelievers. In Muslim law, for example, believers are enjoined not to kill and even to forgive, if they can, those who have done so, but they are also told, "Whoever shall kill a believer purposely, his reward is hell; for ever shall he abide therein" (Roberts, 1925, p. 82). Under Muslim law, believers are punished less severely for the murder of an unbeliever than for that of a believer. Although Christians have not encoded such a measure, history shows vividly that in fact Christians have often regarded the killing of "heathens" as unimportant or even necessary, whereas the same crime against another Christian would be considered heinous.

For students, the most important lesson here is probably one of self-understanding. As they pride themselves on various manifestations of group loyalty, they should also learn to ask themselves hard questions about how to treat strangers, opponents, enemies, and those who are just different. They need to search for the compassionate, inclusionary doctrines in their religions so that, when calls to war or hostility are voiced in the name of religion, they can answer, "But our word also says. . . ." They should also learn to apply compassionate rules of the group to strangers: What if this person were one of ours? Would our judgment be different? Possibly no lesson is more important to learn today than this one—whether the criterion of exclusion be religion, race, ethnicity, gender, or any other group association. What we learn by way of compassion and decency within our special groups is not meant to stop there but to extend into the whole world.

ETHICS AND SOCIAL RESPONSIBILITY

There is, perhaps, an inherent difficulty in trying to extend religious ethics to the whole world. Alasdair MacIntyre (1966) notes:

The paradox of Christian ethics is precisely that it has always tried to devise a code for society as a whole from pronouncements which were addressed to individuals or small communities to separate themselves off from the rest of society. This is true both of the ethics of Jesus and of the ethics of St. Paul. Both Jesus and St. Paul preached an ethics devised for a short interim period before God finally inaugurated the Messianic kingdom and history was brought to a conclusion. We cannot, therefore, expect to find in what they say a basis for life in a continuing society. (p. 115)

In particular, the gentler message of Christianity has often been overwhelmed by the realization that the kingdom is not, in fact, at hand. It is one thing to turn the other cheek and to do good to those who use us spitefully if we are sure that the evil order will soon be overturned; it is quite another when there is no end in sight. When we add to the apparently endless stability of evil the modern mockery of those who proselytize, we can begin to understand why religious adherents often turn to the more militant messages in their traditions.

But, as we have seen, the last century and a half has been characterized by a demand for compassion in religion. Religious ethics have to measure up to secular ethics in their campaign against pain and cruelty. The demand for compassion supported movements like social gospel in the nineteenth century and has led to a revival of interest in charity as fundamental to Christianity. Not everyone agrees with MacIntyre that Christian ethics cannot serve a continuing society. Gustavo Gutierrez (1988) writes:

In the first place, *charity* has been fruitfully rediscovered as the center of the Christian life. This has led to a more Biblical view of the faith as an act of trust, a going out of one's self, a commitment to God and neighbor, a relationship with others. It is in this sense that St. Paul tells us that faith works through charity: love is the nourishment and the fullness of faith, the gift of oneself to the Other, and invariably to others. This is the foundation of the *praxis* of Christians, of their active presence in history. According to the Bible, faith is the total human response to God, who saves through love. In this light, the understanding of the faith appears as the understanding not of the simple affirmation—almost memorization—of truths, but of a commitment, an overall attitude, a particular posture toward life. (p. 6)

The liberation theology of Gutierrez echoes Kung's statement that belief is proved in practice, but it goes well beyond it—making practice primary and belief and reflection secondary. As we have already noted, emphasis on social practice raises problems for institutional religions because their survival often depends on their collaboration with the dominant politics and social ethics. They can exhort their members to live by whatever conventional morality is currently spoken, but they take a great risk in urging anything beyond this. Gutierrez (1988) notes that when priests and other religious work actively for social change, they are considered subversive: "The dissidence of priests and religious . . . appears as particularly dangerous, especially if we consider the role which they have traditionally played" (p. 62).

Liberation theology is not only socially subversive; it is theologically subversive as well—giving new meaning to a host of theological terms. Sin is now described in human terms: "We feel we have a right and a duty to condemn unfair wages, exploitation, and starvation tactics as clear indications of sin and evil" (Gutierrez, 1988, p. 64). Sharon Welch (1985), a feminist theologian, explains further that the concern of liberation theology is

> not sin in a universal sense, but sin in particular, sin as the denial of solidarity. A liberating Christian faith addresses historical conditions of fallenness with a hope for a struggle toward redemption in history. That faith that grounds theologies of liberation is intrinsically historical and particular, directed toward the denunciation and transformation of specific forms of oppression. (p. 27)

Resurrection, too, is given new meaning in liberation theology.

> Resurrection is the most encoded symbol of faith, and it resists decoding. It is the utmost yes to life. . . . The symbol transforms even death into an instrument of life. Different times will attempt different translations of this mystery. While the bourgeois theology emphasized the individual dimension, the new theology . . . will emphasize the social dimension of the mystery. Hence we bring together liberation with resurrection because our deepest need is not personal immortality but a life before death for all human beings. (Soelle, 1978, p. 34; quoted in Welch, 1985, p. 45)

Liberation theology is, thus, a religious humanism. It urges human beings to take responsibility, to act, to transform, and it casts theology in the role of critical theory—a body of reflective thought that analyzes the deepest discontents of an era and the response of believers to those discontents. Gutierrez (1988) writes:

> It is important to keep in mind that beyond—or rather, through—the struggle against misery, injustice, and exploitation the goal is the *creation*

of a new humanity. Vatican II has declared, "We are witnesses of the birth of a new humanism, one in which man is defined first of all by his responsibility toward his brothers and toward history" (*Gaudium et spes.* no. 55). This aspiration to create a new man is the deepest motivation in the struggle which many have undertaken in Latin America. (p. 81)

Gandhi's religious philosophy also led to social action.

> His movement was a return to the humanism of his folk culture and the spirituality of his religion through the literariness of the scriptures. Because they were poetic texts, Gandhi could read them as symbolically charged with contemporary meaning, and satyagraha [nonviolent soul-force] itself is an act of poesis, and act of making, more invention than technique. (Inchausti, 1991, p. 29)

Religious liberatory doctrines can, however, become self-righteous and intolerant of those whose conditions do not yield so easily to prescribed techniques. Gandhi outraged Jewish thinkers by recommending that Jews submit to Nazi atrocities and try to convert their tormentors through love and nonviolence. Martin Buber chastized Gandhi.

> Now, do you know or *do you not* know, Mahatma, what a concentration camp is like and what goes on there? . . . And do you think perhaps that a Jew in Germany could pronounce one single sentence of speech such as yours without being knocked down? . . . In the five years which I myself spent under the present regime, I observed many instances of genuine *satyagraha* among the Jews. . . . Such actions, however, apparently exerted not the slightest influence on their opponents. (quoted in Friedman, 1991, p. 214)

Critics of religious social doctrines may thus find them on occasion too rigid and too unrealistic. But other critics chide or even condemn them because they put too much emphasis on human agency and not enough on God. Some contemporary Christian writings, for example, reflect a more contemplative and mystical attitude toward social action. Service, as a reflection of personal commitment, is seen primarily as a sign of God's compassion working through the humans who serve. Such writers, sometimes saintly in their own conduct, emphasize service and prayer rather than transformative social action.

> The most important resources for counteracting the constant temptation to slip into activism is the knowledge that in Christ everything has

been accomplished. This knowledge should be understood not as an intellectual insight, but as an understanding in faith. As long as we continue to act as if the salvation of the world depends on us, we lack the faith by which mountains can be moved. In Christ, human suffering and pain have already been accepted and suffered. . . . Our action, therefore, must be understood as a discipline by which we make visible what has already been accomplished. (McNeill, Morrison, & Nouwen, 1983, p. 122)

For high school students, discussion of the long-standing tension between social action and individual spirituality can serve at least to shake complacency. When students hear that their conventional acts of charity—"giving to the poor"—can actually be regarded as oppressive acts that tend to keep everything as it is and, thus, to undermine the struggle to end domination, they may well be astonished. But reflection on such discussions may also lead to thoughtful examination of life-styles in the United States, the selfishness of continual striving for more and more material goods, the ways in which religion sometimes soothes our consciences when they should remain disturbed, and the enormous risks taken by a few who are willing to give up both personal and spiritual comfort.

CHAPTER 8

Is Such a Program
Possible in Schools?

What I have described in the preceding seven chapters is so far from the typical content of today's classroom that a question naturally arises whether such exploration is possible in public schools. Even sympathetic readers may wonder about the constitutionality of such teaching, whether the material discussed here should be part of the formal curriculum, whether teachers can be prepared to handle the material sensitively and confidently, whether structural changes would be required in schools if we decide to encourage the program, how educators can meet the objections sure to arise from fundamentalists, and, finally, whether such a program is in fact morally desirable.

CONSTITUTIONAL ISSUES

The constitutionality issue should be easily settled—which is not to say that it will actually be easily settled. Teaching *about* religion has long been accepted. The central problem in the approach I have outlined is that religious or metaphysical questions may arise anywhere, and I have recommended not only that they be treated wherever they arise—in, say, math or physics classes—but that teachers should assume that students are continually asking such questions implicitly, and, therefore, that they should plan their lessons to include such material. Following such a plan means that students will not be able to escape the discussion of religious questions. They will at least hear (even if they decline to participate in) discussions about God, ethics, creation, religious politics, mystical love, atheism, feminism, and a host of other topics. Does this constitute an improper intrusion on their freedom to choose their own attitude toward religion?

Including religious, metaphysical, and existential questions need be no more intrusive than including mathematical or literary questions. Indeed, the approach I have suggested is less intrusive, for I am not recommending that students be tested on the material offered or that their participation in debate be in any way part of their academic evaluation. Such discussions, whether they are initiated by students or teachers, should be part of the free exchange of human concerns—a way in which people striving for intelligent belief or unbelief share their awe, doubts, fears, hopes, knowledge, and ignorance. The school arena in which these exchanges take place will also be one in which students learn to respond to one another with compassion and understanding and also with considerate demands for appropriate levels of logic.

The method of pedagogical neutrality is essential in discussing religious questions. To advocate a particular sectarian view is clearly unconstitutional. But to ignore—as we do now—that people have taken such views and that these views, in many cases, have been enormously influential is morally reprehensible. It will not do to say that such material should be deferred until college. Some students never get to college, and those who do, having had no previous preparation, are in no better position to choose critically than their slightly younger peers. All students deserve an opportunity to engage matters central to life in an environment that is noncoercive and supportive.

Teachers committed to pedagogical neutrality will not say to students whose parents have taught them that the world is only a few thousand years old, "That's wrong." Rather they will acknowledge the fact that some people believe this, and they will lay out what most scientists believe. In doing this, they should admit that there are several conflicting stories within evolution theory itself. In science, too, we find imaginative leaps and creative filling in of gaps. Do any scientists believe that the world was created in six days just a few thousand years ago? The honest answer has to be *very few*. But, we may also honestly add, there are many, many stories of creation—some far stranger than the biblical stories. Should we ask of them that they be literally true, or do they play another role in the quest for human meaning? I'll return to this example when I consider the question of how to deal with fundamentalism, but for now my purpose is to show that teachers need not say, "This is true," or "I believe that. . . . '' They need only refer to beliefs clearly stated by others and let students weigh the evidence or decide consciously to reject it in favor of faith.

CURRICULUM AND PEDAGOGY

The discussion so far suggests that this vital material on belief and unbelief *not* be made a part of the formal curriculum. This is probably the right decision. Anything that becomes part of the formal curriculum is cast far too specifically and rigidly, examined unappreciatively by partisan and sectarian eyes, evaluated by student achievement, and—worst of all—made intolerably boring to all but a handful of students passionately interested in the subject.

My preference would be to include the material as sets of suggestions for enriching and supplementing standard topics. These sets of suggestions would be part of a meta-level of curriculum planning, and teachers would be urged to consider them as they plan lessons and units. In addition, a variety of suggestions would be made in connection with specific topics. For example, in presenting a unit on graphing and the Cartesian coordinate system, teachers would discuss the life of Descartes—his mode of dress, life in his time, his military service, and his attempt to prove that God exists.

But if teachers teach the material, won't they automatically, inexorably, inevitably test on it? And why am I so reluctant to permit testing in this area? It might be permissible to include questions on religious matters as optional: Choose one of the following. Choice of that kind would allow students to show how their thinking is developing and, at least as important, would grant them credit for thinking on this particular material. Providing such choice would show that we take the topics seriously in an official way. But the problems are considerable. Questions designed for tests are likely to be superficial, and the answers may be judged dogmatically even if teachers have maintained pedagogical neutrality in class discussion. Should students be required to demonstrate a form of neutrality in their answers? Should they be evaluated on their capacity to do this? Such a requirement may indeed be intrusive, and it is asking too much of people who do not bear the special moral obligation of teachers.

Further, there ought to be gifts freely given in education. Aristotle once said that teaching does whatever it does "as to a friend." In the discussion of religious, metaphysical, and existential questions, teachers and students are both seekers. Teachers tell stories, guide the logic of discussion, point to further readings, model both critical thinking and kindness, and show by their openness what it means to seek intelligent belief or unbelief. Students long for gifts of this sort from their teachers. Some years ago, when I was a high school mathematics teacher, I read a science fiction story to my geometry class. The hero of the story was a mathematician—a topologist, to be precise. When I finished the reading—which students apparently enjoyed enormously—the first question asked was, "Are we going to be tested on this?" No. "Well, then, why . . . ?" My answer (which embarrassed even me a bit) went something like this: Because it's one of my favorite stories, I like you, and I wanted to share it with you. My students were clearly pleased and just as clearly astonished. Teachers who admit to liking their students? Teachers willing to share something they love—as a gift? Since then, I've often wondered why we do not engage in such activities more frequently.

Most teachers today are not prepared to conduct the kinds of exploration I have described. But they could be. High school teachers should be what we once called "renaissance people"; that is, at an appropriate level, they should know a great deal about most of the subjects taught in secondary schools and, in addition, should be acquainted with a vast volume of connected material. This sort of breadth could be achieved if the undergraduate preparation of teachers was frankly aimed at preparing teachers.

Several influential organizations today recommend a strong liberal arts preparation for teachers (Carnegie Task Force, 1986; Holmes Group, 1986). The idea behind the recommendation is admirable. These educational leaders want teachers to have a broad academic background. But forcing every teacher to complete a standard disciplinary major and the usual hodgepodge of undergraduate studies will not accomplish the desired aim. First, the subject matter major will be too highly specialized to have much relevance to the high school curriculum. Second, most of the required "breadth" courses will be bits of other specialties. None will serve the function of connecting the major with the deep questions we have been exploring.

People who are preparing to teach at the high school level need to study the high school curriculum in great depth. Just as physicians must study anatomy, and lawyers torts, teachers need to study the curriculum. It is the backbone of their work. And the heart of their work is the students who must grapple with this curriculum. Together, teachers and students struggle to find meaning for their lives in this curriculum. Yet the present reality is that most math teachers cannot help their homeroom students with English or history, and most English teachers turn pale at the mention of math problems. Thus the high school emulates the college with its collection of specialists none of whom is charged with the human responsibility to explore religious and existential questions.

It is no longer possible to produce renaissance scholars at the level of university expertise. There is simply too much material to master. But at the high school level, it is possible. Indeed, we assume that it is possible to acquire something close to this level of expertise when we require all students to take certain subjects. If all high school students must take a prescribed set of subjects, then surely it is not unreasonable to insist that all high school teachers should know this material quite well. After all, they went through it themselves as high school students and, I am suggesting, they should have studied it again from a higher standpoint in college. Teaching is the one profession for which it makes sense to be a renaissance scholar. Just imagine how much greater students' respect for their teachers might be, if schools were staffed by such people!

The objection might be raised that such preparation would require that people identify teaching as their goal upon entry to college. True. But engineering students are also required to make their choice early, so teachers would not be unique. What if they changed their minds? Lots of people do. They would still have had a fine, general education—possibly better than the liberal arts as snippets of specialties that we now offer. It is odd that we worry more about people changing their minds than we do about people ''preparing'' for careers in ways largely irrelevant to their current choices. Under the plan I am suggesting here, students would study material directly relevant to their career choice. Even if that choice changes, they will have learned what it feels like to be fully engaged—to pursue studies with an aim, to be taught in a way that acknowledges the value and dignity of their chosen profession.

But math teachers would, then, not know as much math as those who intend to study math in graduate school. It is true that they would not have the same facility with real analysis and topology. But the budding mathematician will not be familiar with the biographical, historical, and other connections that the teacher will have mastered. Further, math teachers today do not have the mathematical facility of graduate students in mathematics. Because they do not use that kind of mathematics in their daily work, they forget it, and at present they rarely compensate for the loss by acquiring the knowledge I have alluded to. If teachers were prepared as I am suggesting, we would not have to answer the perennial question, ''What do teachers know that others trained in the same subject do not know?'' with unconvincing bits of ''pedagogical'' knowledge. We could point to a vast body of material they know that others have never mastered or have long ago forgotten.

A substantial segment of preparation would be devoted to the connections of the standard subjects to the religious and existential questions we have been discussing. Other segments would be devoted to vocational, recreational, and developmental issues (Noddings, 1992). Students and their interests and needs would govern how the curriculum is organized and presented. It is obvious that teachers would have to master the entire curriculum so conceived— not just tiny portions of it.

When we face teacher preparation with complete practicality, we know the suggestions just made are unlikely to be implemented. Sadly, high school teachers will not be prepared over the full range of required subjects (nor will the requirements be dropped, although this alternative is perhaps even more attractive and defensible than the one I've outlined above; see Noddings, 1992). The only practical possibility is to include much of the material discussed in earlier chapters in a professional preparation program and to encourage teachers to continue their own truly liberal education.

Professional programs must make it clear to teachers that the study and discussion of religious and existential questions is legitimate. I would even say that such discussion is morally obligatory. The discussion of values at every level and in every familiar human context is essential. As David Purpel (1989) puts it:

> As educators, . . . , our responsibilities are not to promulgate visions but to inquire into them, not just to study them but to be critical and discerning of them. . . . Hence, we cannot in good educational conscience avoid the serious and volatile disputes on religious and moral matters because they are controversial, complex, and outrageously perplexing. Quite the contrary: *because* they are so important and *since* they beg for awareness, understanding, clarification, and insight, they are central to significant educational inquiry. (p. 68)

With such an understanding of our pedagogical obligation, we can at least supply student teachers with knowledge of ''how to do it.'' Unfortunately, they will have to acquire much of the content on their own.

It would be helpful if teachers had the kind of education that would enable them to make connections across subject fields and to discuss deep human questions with some sophistication. But, more important than preparation on specific content, teachers need to be released from the taboos that keep all of us from exploring the questions that matter most deeply to us. It is an odd society that shrugs off the influence of violence, steamy sex, and greed displayed daily on television, and worries, instead, that its children will be corrupted by the free discussion of controversial issues in school. This is not to say that there should be no concern over such discussions. There should be constant concern. Parents should be deeply involved in these discussions, but they should not obstruct or prevent them from occurring.

Both parents and students need to have trust in the teachers who lead such discussions, and trust is cultivated slowly as caring relations are established. Trust is not automatically conferred on those who present appropriate credentials. As parents, most of us begin to trust when we are convinced that a particular teacher really does have the best interests of our child at heart. As we see our child grow intellectually, socially, and morally, our trust deepens. We will allow—even encourage—a teacher we trust to broach highly sensitive subjects.

The need for trust suggests that students and teachers should stay together for more than the usual one year. One of the great strengths of many independent schools is exactly this—that teachers do follow their students over a period of years and take considerable responsibility for their full growth. Ideally, the choice to remain together should be mutual, for dislike of a teacher is unlikely to be transformed into trust by forced association. We are all familiar with the dark side of the independent school arrangement in which one teacher (or master) can make the lives of some students miserable for years. The positive possibilities of such a plan are also familiar to us in the influence of public school coaches and other teachers. Often an athletic coach or music teacher works with students (who *choose* athletics or music) for a period of several years, and these people are able to build relations of trust that enable them to discuss matters that other teachers are afraid to touch.

Prolonged association and the expectation that teachers will engage their students in controversial and sensitive discussion put tremendous responsibility on teachers. On the one hand, because students will do all sorts of things for people they love and trust, the ordinary tasks of teaching become easier. There is no need to concoct a continuous stream of flashy lessons meant to motivate recalcitrant students. On the other hand, a thoughtless or unethical teacher can lead students into foolish, corrupt, dangerous, and even tragic acts.

Readers may recall the teacher in *All Quiet on the Western Front* who convinced his young students that it was glorious to fight and die for the fatherland. *En masse,* the boys left the schoolroom to join up, and almost all eventually were killed. But we cannot prevent tragedy and foolishness by accepting structures that make it impossible for relations of trust to develop. We cannot satisfy existential longings by pretending they do not exist. We cannot excuse ourselves from the responsibility to meet these longings in school by saying that we would approve the suggested program if our children could have the very best teachers. Just as most children have to be satisfied with "good enough" parents, so we will have to work with "good enough" teachers. Teachers who care deeply for their students, who are willing to engage in continuous inquiry, and who are committed to pedagogical neutrality are probably good enough. It is also possible that teachers, as well as students, will grow from "good enough" to considerably better under a program that allows full discussion of religious and ethical values.

IS CRITICAL ANALYSIS POSSIBLE IN SCHOOLS?

In the past few years, educators have been repeatedly frustrated in attempts to introduce "values education." Public reaction is often negative because each faction in the community fears that the values of some other group will dominate. Some even proclaim rather self-righteously that they do not want to impose their own values on others. But teaching in the domain of values need not be dogmatic any more than the teaching of mathematics need be conducted by rote and drill. The answer to the stubborn question, "Whose values?" has to be something like this: In a sense *everyone's.* We do not intentionally teach any values without critical examination. As we question and explore, we may indeed discover shared values, and certainly we will discover deep individual commitments. Values that express treasured commitments will be examined both critically and appreciatively. When we say that we stand for something in this community, that we will not tolerate some forms of behavior, that we put high value on other forms, we mean that those of us so committed have examined our beliefs and ways of life and have decided to live by these values—even though different members of the community may refer to different underlying or deep values, and many of us acknowledge that both the deep values and surface values may change sometime in the future.

Such ongoing analysis allows both commitment and doubt. It does not arrogantly assume that all decent, well-behaved members of the community are decent and well behaved because of their shared religious convictions, nor would it callously allow the dominant religious orientation to establish itself as a pseudo-universal. Martin Buber (1967) described the pain he experienced as a Jewish schoolboy undergoing the usual Christian morning exercises.

> The obligatory daily standing in the room resounding with the strange service affected me worse than an act of intolerance could have affected me. Compulsory guests, having to participate as a thing in a sacral event in which no dram of my person could or would take part, and this for eight long years morning after morning: that stamped itself upon the life-substance of the boy. (p. 8)

Even today there are many in this country who would like to restore the old morning exercises—Bible reading, Lord's prayer, and flag salute. We should be firm in resisting this demand. Devout believers can engage in their devotions with communities of believers in houses of worship. Those whose beliefs differ must not be made unwilling participants or "things," as Buber described his own role, at ceremonies foreign or obnoxious to them. Why not? How do "we" come to hold this value? Some of us honestly believe that prayer in public school has rightly been declared unconstitutional, others fear that nondenominational exercises will rapidly slide over into overtly denominational ones, and still others simply want to preserve all children from the pain experienced by Buber.

Teachers and parents who resist every form of values education because they do not wish to impose their own values on others cannot have examined their practices critically. Do they insist that children attend school? that they be punctual in attendance at all classes? that they complete assignments on time? that they listen to their teachers—or, at least, do not interfere with their teachers' speech? that they not use racial epithets or obscene language in class? Every rule is based on some value, and obedience to rules suggests some underlying belief—even if it is only the intellectually impoverished belief in following rules. Thus, like it or not, we do impose our values on the young and the subordinate, but we can avoid doing so dogmatically. We can give reasons, encourage questions, and abandon rules that do not stand up under critical examination.

The biggest stumbling block to educating for intelligent belief or unbelief is probably fundamentalism and all those linguistic practices implicitly associated with it. We profess the fear that teachers do not have the competence to teach the required material, but a considerable number of practicing teachers of mathematics do not have the mathematical competence of a proficient high school calculus student. Yet we do not abandon mathematics teaching. Mathematics is important (although not so important that everyone should be required to study algebra), and we keep trying to improve both teaching and curriculum. An acknowledgment of the importance of intelligent belief or unbelief should induce similar efforts. The real problem is that some vocal people do not put a high value on intelligence in matters of religion and even judge critical examination of belief to be a form of sin (Peshkin, 1986). Sin dominates the interests of fundamentalists. Harold Bloom (1992) comments on the sins defined by Jimmy Swaggart.

> "Abortion, atheism, evolution, communism, liberalism, infanticide, euthanasia, ERA, homosexuality, lesbianism, and perversion." Evidently Swaggart does not know the differences among these eleven "sins," though presumably it was not "liberalism" he sought in some of his wanderings. (p. 178)

Surely we want our students to analyze the concepts Swaggart so easily labels "sin" and form intelligent opinions about each. Educators need to respond to efforts at censorship and curtailment of debate with courage and compassion. Not only does the full development of each individual human being depend on rational discussion of controversial issues but so does the health of our democracy. As Amy Gutmann (1987) puts it: "Because conscious social reproduction is the primary ideal of democratic education, communities must be prevented from using education to stifle rational deliberation" (p. 45).

Christian fundamentalism today presents a formidable paradox. On the one hand, it insists on its own unique and certain grasp of absolutes; on the other, it insists that these certainties must be accepted without critical examination. Again, on the one hand, it resists a social mission for the church, insisting that the church's job is to preach the gospel and save souls. On the other, it has become politically active and seeks to convert the nation. James Barr (1977) notes the latter paradox.

> The claim of the evangelical gospel to be a radical questioning of the inner bases of human self-certainty is suddenly reversed, when the religion becomes the ideological guarantor of the rightness of the exist-

ing order. . . . Evangelicalism of this kind is seen to hanker for a traditional and more or less medieval Christendom, a Christian country dominated by Christian values, using its military power in knightly style against the enemies of God. (p. 110)

Noting that many fundamentalists use the Bible as a prop, reading from it only rarely and selectively, Barr (1977) also comments on the first paradox.

The ecumenical problem is constituted by the frightening alienation of fundamentalism from the main stream of church life and theology. . . . At the root of the problem there lies . . . a judgment that is more religious and existential than doctrinal or biblical: the problem is formed by the absolute and overweening certainty possessed by fundamentalists that their form of religion is absolutely and uniquely right. (p. 338)

As Barr describes it, fundamentalism is not an intellectual problem because there is nothing intellectual in it. But public schools have, among other worthy aims, intellectual aims, and the only legitimate way for schools to enter domains of life such as religion is intellectual. Most nonfundamentalist religions acknowledge the intellectual dimension of religion, even though they may insist that faith is more a matter of the heart than of the head. Indries Shah (1970), capturing the spirit of Sufism and, we might say, of all intelligent religious practice, quotes Ali.

You probably seem to yourself to be a believer, even if you are a believer in disbelief. But you cannot really believe in anything until you are aware of the process by which you arrived at your position. Before you do this you must be ready to postulate that all your beliefs may be wrong, that what you think to be belief may only be a variety of prejudice caused by your surroundings—including the bequest of your ancestors for whom you may have a sentiment. (p. 164)

It is exactly this attitude that school discussion should further, and, of course, it is exactly this attitude that fundamentalism opposes.

I am willing to argue that a critical and appreciative examination of religion belongs in schools and that the vast majority of students would profit from it. But we must consider whether critical thinking is in itself an invasion of the religious privacy of fundamentalists. Does such educational effort abridge the rights of fundamentalists to practice their religion? Will education of the sort recommended here endanger faith?

Education, even if it does not treat religion explicitly, always endangers blind faith, but it does not necessarily destroy belief; it may indeed deepen it. However, our courts have recognized the danger that schooling presents to faith and, in at least the case of the Amish, have permitted a religious community to limit the education of its children. Debate still occurs over the wisdom of this decision. Is religion thus protected through the deprivation of children? Without pursuing this interesting question, we can observe that the Amish do not assert that all people should follow their practices, nor do they try to impose their values through political action. If they did, we would have to respond to them as I think we must to fundamentalists: You are free to practice your religion as you see fit, but when you enter the public arena, your commitments and recommendations must be and will be subjected to the methods of intelligence. The public school is committed to these methods, and your children will necessarily encounter them.

As Purpel (1989) put it, we cannot in "good educational conscience" avoid the application of critical intelligence to matters of religion and value, but our good conscience should not drive us to demean the beliefs of fundamentalist students. It should be acknowledged that some fundamentalist beliefs—such as the one that God loves each of us individually—are widely shared in mainstream religions and, simultaneously, widely doubted. Those who do not claim fundamentalist affiliation may be surprised to learn how deeply our American society and our patterns of moral speech have been affected by fundamentalism (Bloom, 1992).

In considering how to treat fundamentalism with genuine respect for its adherents and firm consistency in light of our commitment to intelligence, I want to return to the earlier discussion of creation and evolution. Clearly, it is not intelligent to censor or proscribe full discussion of any view passionately held by one or more participant. To approach questions about our origins intelligently, we should tell the full story as nearly as we can. All cultures have creation stories, and telling them or encouraging students to find and tell them presents a wonderful opportunity for multicultural education. Here our predilection for dichotomies and other rigidly marked categories leads us to insist that, if those stories be told at all, they be included in literature or history class—not science. It would be far better if our studies were not organized along these arbitrary disciplinary lines (Noddings, 1992), but as long as they are, intelligent educators must be willing to cross the lines. Science teachers should begin by acknowledging the eternal human quest for solutions to the puzzle of our existence. As science teachers, they have a special obligation to pass on to students the most widely accepted contemporary beliefs in science together with the evidence used to support them. But as educators, they have an even greater responsibility to acknowledge and present with great sensitivity the full range of solutions explored by their fellow human beings. Again, such discussions do not have to end with, "Now here's the truth." The best teachers will be prepared to present not only the full spectrum of belief but also the variety of plausible ways in which people have tried to reconcile their religious and scientific beliefs.

In both science and education today, we are beginning to understand the fragility of facts—those peculiar statements wrenched free of context and speaker. It seems far wiser to say, "Here's what we've learned so far," than to state a string of propositions cold. Further, we then have to explain who "we" are, how we learned what we're disclosing, and what our purposes were when we set out to inquire. In education, we have come to appreciate "a good story and a well-formed argument" (Makler, 1991). When we try to educate for intelligent belief or unbelief, we must draw on a multitude of stories and use our best style of argumentation. The purpose is not to defeat an antagonist—certainly not to shatter another's belief—but to provide all participants with an opportunity to think things through and to participate in that eternal dialogue of which we spoke in Chapter 5. In such a dialogue, believer and unbeliever draw closer to one another. Thoughtful Christians, Jews, Confucianists, Sufis, humanists—all recognize our dependence on human goodness and compassion. In the words of a Sufi teaching, "Sin against God is one thing; but sinning against man is worse" (Shah, 1970, p. 163). To understand this is one great aim of educating for intelligent belief or unbelief.

References

Abbott, Edwin A. (1952). *Flatland*. New York: Dover. (Original work published 1884)

Albanese, Catherine L. (1991). *Nature religion in America: From the Algonkian Indians to the new age*. Chicago and London: University of Chicago Press.

Aries, Philippe. (1981). *The hour of our death*. New York: Alfred A. Knopf.

Bain, F. W. (1911). *The ashes of a God*. New York: G. P. Putnam's Sons.

Baldwin, James. (1953). *Go tell it on the mountain*. New York: Dell.

Barnes, Hazel E. (1974). *The meddling gods*. Lincoln: University of Nebraska Press.

Barnes, Hazel E. (1978). *An existentialist ethics*. Chicago: University of Chicago Press.

Barr, James. (1977). *Fundamentalism*. Philadelphia: Westminster Press.

Barrett, William. (1962). *Irrational man: A study in existential philosophy*. Garden City, NY: Anchor Books.

Baudrillard, Jean. (1990). *Fatal strategies* (P. Beitchman & W. G. J. Niesluchowski, Trans.; J. Fleming, Ed.). New York: Semiotext(e).

Becher, Jeanne. (Ed.). (1990). *Women, religion and sexuality*. Philadelphia: Trinity Press International.

Bell, E. T. (1965). *Men of mathematics*. New York: Simon & Schuster. (Original work published 1937)

Bellah, Robert N., Madsen, Richard, Sullivan, William M., Swidler, Ann, & Tipton, Steven M. (1985). *Habits of the heart*. Berkeley and Los Angeles: University of California Press.

Benhabib, Seyla. (1987). The generalized and the concrete other. In S. Benhabib & D. Cornell (Eds.), *Feminism as critique* (pp. 77-95). Minneapolis: University of Minnesota Press.

Bird, Phyllis. (1974). Images of women in the Old Testament. In R. R. Ruether (Ed.), *Religion and sexism* (pp. 41-88). New York: Simon & Schuster.

Bleeker, C. F. (1963). Isis as saviour goddess. In S. G. F. Brandon (Ed.), *The saviour God: Comparative studies in the concept of salvation* (pp. 1-16). Manchester, England: University of Manchester Press.

Bloom, Harold. (1992). *The American religion: The emergence of the post-Christian nation*. New York: Simon & Schuster.

Brandon, S. G. F. (1963). The ritual technique of salvation in the ancient Near East. In S. G. F. Brandon (Ed.), *The saviour God: Comparative studies in the concept of salvation* (pp. 17–36). Manchester, England: University of Manchester Press.

Braunthal, Alfred. (1979). *Salvation and the perfect society*. Amherst: University of Massachusetts Press.

Buber, Martin. (1967). Autobiographical fragments. In P. Schilpp & M. Friedman (Eds.), *The philosophy of Martin Buber* (pp. 3–39). LaSalle, IL: Open Court.

Buck, Pearl S. (1936). *The exile*. New York: Triangle.

Butterworth, Hezekiah. (1875). *The story of the hymns*. New York: American Tract Society.

Carnegie Task Force on Teaching as a Profession. (1986). *A nation prepared*. New York: Carnegie Forum on Education and the Economy.

Cave, Floyd A. (1946). Religion and politics. In J. S. Roucek (Ed.), *20th century political thought* (pp. 171–196). New York: Philosophical Library.

Chomsky, Noam. (1972). *Language and mind*. New York: Harcourt Brace Jovanovich.

Christ, Carol P. (1982). Why women need the goddess: Phenomenological, psychological, and political reflections. In C. Spretnak (Ed.), *The politics of women's spirituality* (pp. 71–86). Garden City, NY: Anchor Books.

Cooey, Paula M., Farmer, Sharon A., & Ross, Mary Ellen (Eds.). (1987). *Embodied love: Sensuality and relationship as feminist values*. San Francisco: Harper & Row.

Daly, Mary. (1974). *Beyond God the father*. Boston: Beacon Press.

Daly, Mary. (1984). *Pure lust*. Boston: Beacon Press.

Davies, Paul. (1983). *God and the new physics*. London: J. M. Dent & Sons, Ltd.

Dewey, John. (1934). *A common faith*. New Haven: Yale University Press.

Dijkstra, Bram. (1986). *Idols of perversity: Fantasies of feminine evil in fin-de-siecle culture*. New York and Oxford: Oxford University Press.

Downing, Christine. (1984). *The goddess*. New York: Crossroad.

DuBois, W. E. B. (1978). *On sociology and the black community* (D. S. Green & E. D. Driver, Eds.). Chicago: University of Chicago Press.

Ehrenreich, Barbara. (1989). Religious values undermine democracy. In J. S. Bach & T. Modl (Eds.), *Religion in America* (pp. 77–85). San Diego: Greenhaven.

Farley, Wendy. (1990). *Tragic vision and divine compassion: A contemporary theodicy*. Louisville, KY: Westminster/John Knox Press.

Fosdick, Harry Emerson. (1961). Old and new ideas of God. In *In Search of God and immortality* (pp. 72–90). Boston: Beacon Press.

Fowler, James W. (1991). *Weaving the new creation: Stages of faith and the public church*. San Francisco: Harper.

Freud, Sigmund. (1939). *Moses and monotheism*. New York: Vintage Books.

Friedman, Maurice. (1991). *Encounter on the narrow ridge: A life of Martin Buber.* New York: Paragon House.

Gardner, Martin. (1983). *The whys of a philosophical scrivener.* New York: Quill.

Gibson, Arthur. (1969). *The silence of God: Creative response to the films of Ingmar Bergman.* New York: Harper & Row.

Greene, Maxine. (1978). *Landscapes of learning.* New York: Teachers College Press.

Grenier, Richard. (1983). *The Gandhi nobody knows.* Nashville: Thomas Nelson.

Griffin, David Lee. (1991). *Evil revisited.* Albany: State University of New York Press.

Grimshaw, Patricia. (1983). 'Christian woman, pious wife, faithful mother, devoted missionary': Conflicts in roles of American missionary women in nineteenth-century Hawaii. *Feminist Studies, 9*(3), 489–522.

Gutierrez, Gustavo. (1988). *A theology of liberation.* Maryknoll, NY: Orbis Books.

Gutmann, Amy. (1987). *Democratic education.* Princeton: Princeton University Press.

Harding, M. Esther. (1976). *Woman's mysteries.* New York: Harper Colophon Books.

Hassan, Riffat. (1990). An Islamic perspective. In J. Becher (Ed.), *Women, religion and sexuality* (pp. 93–128). Philadelphia: Trinity Press International.

Hauerwas, Stanley. (1983). On keeping theological ethics theological. In S. Hauerwas & A. MacIntyre (Eds.), *Revisions: Changing perspectives in moral philosophy* (pp. 16–42). Notre Dame, IN: University of Notre Dame Press.

Hauerwas, Stanley, & MacIntyre, Alasdair. (Eds.). (1983). *Revisions: Changing perspectives in moral philosophy.* Notre Dame, IN: University of Notre Dame Press.

Haught, James A. (1990). *Holy horrors.* Buffalo, NY: Prometheus Press.

Heard, Gerald. (1961). Death and consciousness. In *In search of God and immortality* (pp. 45–71). Boston: Beacon Press.

Hentoff, N. (1992, June). Letter to the editor. *Village Voice.*

Hick, John. (1966). *Evil and the God of love.* London: Macmillan.

Hoffer, Eric. (1951). *The true believer.* New York: Harper & Row.

Hofstadter, Douglas R. (1979). *Gödel, Escher, Bach: An eternal golden braid.* New York: Basic Books.

Hofstadter, Douglas R. (1985). *Metamagical themes: Questing for the essence of mind and pattern.* New York: Basic Books.

Holmes Group. (1986). *Tomorrow's teachers.* East Lansing, MI: Author.

Hook, Sidney. (1961). Conflicting conceptions of God. In *In search of God and immortality* (pp. 120–141). Boston: Beacon Press.

Hubbard, Ruth. (1979). Have only men evolved? In R. Hubbard, M. S. Henefin, & B. Fried (Eds.), *Women look at biology looking at women* (pp. 17–46). Cambridge, MA: Schenkman.

Inchausti, Robert. (1991). *The ignorant perfection of ordinary people.* Albany: State University of New York Press.

James, William. (1899). *The will to believe: And other essays in popular philosophy.* New York: Longman Green.

James, William. (1958). *The varieties of religious experience.* New York: Mentor. (Original work published 1902)

Jung, Carl G. (1969). *Collected works* (Vol. 2, 2nd ed.). Princeton: Princeton University Press.

Jung, Carl G. (1973). *Answer to Job.* (R. F. C. Hull, Trans.). Princeton: Princeton University Press.

Kant, Immanuel. (1966). *Critique of pure reason.* (F. M. Muller, Trans.). New York: Doubleday Anchor Books. (Original work published 1781)

Keller, Evelyn Fox. (1983). *A feeling for the organism: The life and work of Barbara McClintock.* New York: Freeman & Co.

Keller, Evelyn Fox. (1985). *Reflections on gender and science.* New Haven: Yale University Press.

Kinsley, David. (1989). *The goddesses' mirror.* Albany: State University of New York Press.

Kirk, Russell. (1989). Religious values pressure democracy. In J. S. Bach & T. Modl (Eds.), *Religion in America* (pp. 69–76). San Diego: Greenhaven.

Klaits, Joseph. (1985). *Servants of satan.* Bloomington: Indiana University Press.

Kohlberg, Lawrence. (1981). *The philosophy of moral development.* San Francisco: Harper & Row.

Kung, Hans. (1980). *Does God exist?* Garden City, NY: Doubleday.

Kung, Hans. (1990). *Theology for the third millennium.* New York: Doubleday/Anchor.

Kushner, Harold. (1981). *When bad things happen to good people.* New York: Schocken Books.

Lara, Adair. (1992, March 3). Death comes to dinner. *San Francisco Chronicle,* p. E-10.

Levy, Leonard W. (1986). *The establishment clause: Religion and the first amendment.* New York: Macmillan.

Lewis, C. S. (1976). *A grief observed.* Toronto: Bantam.

Lickona, Thomas. (1991). *Educating for character: How our schools can teach respect and responsibility.* New York: Bantam Books.

Lindberg, David C., & Numbers, Ronald L. (Eds.). (1986). *God & nature.* Berkeley: University of California Press.

MacIntyre, Alasdair. (1966). *A short history of ethics.* New York: Macmillan.

MacIntyre, Alasdair. (1984). *After virtue.* Notre Dame, IN: University of Notre Dame Press.

Makler, Andra. (1991). Imagining history: "A good story and a well-formed argument." In C. Witherell & N. Noddings (Eds.), *Stories lives tell* (pp. 29–47). New York: Teachers College Press.

McLaughlin, Eleanor Commo. (1974). Equality of souls, inequality of sexes: Women in medieval theology. In R. R. Ruether (Ed.), *Religion and sexism* (pp. 213–266). New York: Simon & Schuster.

McNeill, Donald P., Morrison, Douglas A., & Nouwen, Henry J. M. (1983). *Compassion: A reflection on the Christian life.* Garden City, NY: Doubleday/ Image.

Mead, Margaret. (1961). Differing concepts of immortality. In *In search of God and immortality* (pp. 91–99). Boston: Beacon Press.

Midgley, Mary. (1984). *Wickedness.* London: Routledge & Kegan Paul.

Miller, Alice. (1983). *For your own good.* (H. Hannun & H. Hannun, Trans.). New York: Farrar-Strauss-Giroux.

Miller, Arthur. (1987). *Timebends.* New York: Grove Press.

Nathanson, Jerome. (1963). Sixty-six million Americans do not belong in any church: What do they believe? In L. Rosten (Ed.), *Religions in America* (pp. 212–218). New York: Simon & Schuster.

Neuman, Abraham A. (1961). A Jewish viewpoint. In *In search of God and immortality* (pp. 1–26). Boston: Beacon Press.

Nietzsche, Friedrich. (1956). *The birth of tragedy.* (F. Golffing, Trans.). Garden City, NY: Doubleday.

Nishida, Kitarō. (1990). *An inquiry into the good.* (M. Abe & C. Ives, Trans.). New Haven: Yale University Press.

Noddings, Nel. (1984). *Caring: A feminine approach to ethics and moral education.* Berkeley: University of California Press.

Noddings, Nel. (1989). *Women and evil.* Berkeley: University of California Press.

Noddings, Nel. (1992). *The challenge to care in schools.* New York: Teachers College Press.

Novak, Michael. (1965). *Belief and unbelief.* New York: Macmillan.

Numbers, Ronald L. (1986). The creationists. In D. C. Lindberg & R. L. Numbers (Eds.), *God & nature.* Berkeley: University of California Press.

Nussbaum, Martha C. (1986). *The fragility of goodness.* Cambridge: Cambridge University Press.

Oakley, Mary Ann B. (1972). *Elizabeth Cady Stanton.* Brooklyn, NY: Feminist Press.

Oliner, Samuel P., & Oliner, Pearl M. (1988). *The altruistic personality: Rescuers of Jews in Nazi Europe.* New York: Free Press.

Orwell, George. (1949). *Nineteen eighty-four.* New York: Harcourt, Brace and World.

Pascal, Blaise. (1966). *Pensees.* (A. J. Krailsheimer, Trans.). Baltimore: Penguin Books. (Original work published 1662)

Payne, Robert. (1969). *The life and death of Mahatma Gandhi.* New York: E. P. Dutton.

Peck, M. S. (1983). *People of the lie.* New York: Simon & Schuster.

Peshkin, Alan. (1986). *God's choice: The total world of a fundamentalist Christian school.* Chicago: University of Chicago Press.

Phillips, John Anthony. (1984). *Eve: The history of an idea.* San Francisco: Harper & Row.

Poincare, Henri. (1956). Mathematical creation. In J. R. Newman (Ed.), *The world of mathematics* (pp. 2041–2050). New York: Simon & Schuster.

Purpel, David E. (1989). *The moral and spiritual crisis in education*. New York: Bergin & Garvey.

Rawls, John. (1971). *A theory of justice*. Cambridge, MA: Harvard University Press.

Ricoeur, Paul. (1969). *The symbolism of evil*. Boston: Beacon Press.

Roberts, Robert. (1925). *The social laws of the Qoran*. London: Williams and Norgate, Ltd.

Robinson, Henry Morton. (1952). *The cardinal*. New York: Pocket Books Cardinal Edition.

Rodger, Alex R. (1982). *Education and faith in an open society*. Edinburgh: Hardsel Press.

Rorty, Richard. (1989). *Contingency, irony, and solidarity*. Cambridge: Cambridge University Press.

Rosten, Leo. (Ed.). (1963). *Religions in America*. New York: Simon & Schuster.

Rucker, Rudy. (1982). *Infinity and the mind*. Boston: Birkhauser.

Ruddick, Sara. (1980). Maternal thinking. *Feminist studies, 6*(2), 342-367.

Ruddick, Sara. (1989). *Maternal thinking: Toward a politics of peace*. Boston: Beacon Press.

Ruether, Rosemary Radford. (1974). Misogynism and virginal feminism in the fathers of the church. In R. R. Ruether (Ed.), *Religion and sexism* (pp. 150-183). New York: Simon & Schuster.

Ruland, Vernon. (1985). *Eight sacred horizons: The religious imagination East and West*. New York: Macmillan.

Russell, Bertrand. (1957). *Why I am not a Christian, and other essays on religion and related subjects*. New York: Simon & Schuster.

Russell, Bertrand. (1963). What is an agnostic? In L. Rosten (Ed.), *Religions in America* (pp. 195-203). New York: Simon & Schuster.

Sagan, Eli. (1988). *Freud, women, and morality: The psychology of good and evil*. New York: Basic Books.

Sartre, Jean-Paul. (1977). *Essays in existentialism*. (W. Baskin, Ed.). Secaucus, NJ: Citadel Press.

Scheffler, Israel. (1960). *The language of education*. Springfield, IL: Charles C. Thomas.

Schilpp, Paul, & Friedman, Maurice. (Eds.). (1967). *The philosophy of Martin Buber*. LaSalle, IL: Open Court.

Schopenhauer, Arthur. (1976). On the suffering in the world. In T. B. Saunders (Ed. and Trans.). *Studies in pessimism*. London: Swan Sonnenschein. (Original work published 1893)

Shah, Indries. (1970). *The way of the Sufi*. New York: E. P. Dutton.

Silber, John. (1989). *Straight shooting: What's wrong with America and how to fix it*. New York: Harper & Row.

Skinner, B. F. (1962). *Walden two*. New York: Macmillan.

Skinner, Tom. (1970). *How black is the gospel?* Philadelphia & New York: J. B. Lippincott.

Smith, D. Howard. (1963). Saviour gods in Chinese religion. In S. G. F.

Brandon (Ed.), *The saviour God: Comparative studies in the concept of salvation* (pp. 174–190). Manchester, England: University of Manchester Press.

Smith, Page. (1984). *The rise of industrial America.* New York: McGraw-Hill.

Soelle, Dorothee. (1978). *Beyond mere dialogue: On being Christian and socialist.* Detroit: American Christians Toward Socialism.

Spencer, Herbert. (1909). *First principles of a new system of philosophy.* New York: D. Appleton. (Original work published 1873)

Spender, Dale. (1980). *Man made language.* London: Routledge & Kegan Paul.

Spretnak, Charlene (Ed.). (1982). *The politics of women's spirituality.* Garden City, NY: Anchor Books.

Starhawk. (1982). Witchcraft as goddess religion. In C. Spretnak (Ed.), *The politics of women's spirituality* (pp. 49–56). Garden City, NY: Anchor Books.

Stark, Rodney, & Bainbridge, William Sims. (1985). *The future of religion.* Berkeley: University of California Press.

Stone, Merlin. (1976). *When God was a woman.* New York: Dial Press.

Strauss, David Friedrich. (1846). *The life of Jesus critically examined.* London: Chapman Brothers.

Swidler, Leonard. (1974). Is sexism a sign of decadence in religion? In J. Plaskow & J. Arnold (Eds.), *Women and religion* (pp. 166–175). Missoula, MT: Scholars Press.

Taylor, Rodney L. (1989). Compassion, caring, and the religious response to suffering. In R. Taylor & W. Watson (Eds.), *They shall not hurt* (pp. 11–32). Boulder: Colorado Associated University Press.

Tierney, Kevin. (1979). *Darrow: A biography.* New York: Thomas Y. Crowell.

Tillich, Paul. (1952). *The courage to be.* New Haven: Yale University Press.

Tolstaya, Tatyana. (1991, April 11). In cannibalistic times [Review of *The great turn: A reassessment* by Robert Conquest]. *The New York Review of Books,* pp. 3–6.

Turner, Frederick. (1991). *Rebirth of value: Meditations on beauty, ecology, religion, and education.* Albany: State University of New York Press.

Turner, James. (1985). *Without God, without creed.* Baltimore: Johns Hopkins University Press.

Twain, Mark. (1982). *Mississippi writings.* New York: Literary Classics of the United States. (Original work published 1885)

Unamuno, Miguel De. (1954). *Tragic sense of life.* (J. E. C. Flitch, Trans.). New York: Dover.

Vandenberg, Donald. (1983). *Human rights in education.* New York: Philosophical Library.

Vogt, Carl. (1969). *Lectures on man: His place in creation, and in the history of the earth.* (J. Hunt, Ed.). London: Longman Green. (Original work published 1864)

Warner, Marina. (1976). *Alone of all her sex.* New York: Alfred A. Knopf.

Welch, Sharon D. (1985). *Communities of resistance and solidarity.* Maryknoll, NY: Orbis Books.

Wiesel, Elie. (1960). *Night*. (S. Rodway, Trans.). New York: Hill and Wang.
Wilson, A. N. (1991). *Against religion*. London: Chatto & Winders.
Wittgenstein, Ludwig. (1971). *Tractatus logico-philosophicus*. London: Rout-
   ledge & Kegan Paul. (Original work published 1922)
Zaehner, R. C. (1974). *Our savage god: The perverse use of eastern thought*. New
   York: Sheed and Ward.

Index

About the Author

Nel Noddings is Lee L. Jacks Professor of Education at Stanford University. She is the author of *Caring: A Feminine Approach to Ethics and Moral Education, Women and Evil, Awakening the Inner Eye: Intuition and Education* (with Paul Shore), *The Challenge to Care in Schools: An Alternative Approach to Education,* and more than one hundred articles on topics ranging from the ethics of care to mathematical problem solving.

DATE DUE

Printed in the United States
34115LVS00005B/61-252